Selective Immigration

Selective Immigration

By
JAMES J. DAVIS
Secretary of Labor

SCOTT·MITCHELL PUBLISHING CO.
ST. PAUL, MINNESOTA

803 Man hattan Bldg

PRINTED IN U. S. A.

PREFACE

This book, discussing the alien in the United States, his relations with our country and our people, and the relations of our people with his, is written in a spirit of sympathy with the man or woman who comes to us from abroad, seeking America as the land of freedom and opportunity. It is submitted to the American people as a statement of basic facts, upon which there may be formed an intelligent public opinion regarding the problem of the alien as an immigrant and as a resident of the United States. The material in the following chapters was originally prepared two years ago for serial publication and is here presented in book form in response to a public demand for a permanent reference work. Since its first publication strides have been taken by legislative and administrative action toward accomplishing the ideal which is advocated; nevertheless there is room for further improvement through legislative enactments, and it is hoped that this book will show the need for the further development of a definite policy on the part of our Government as to immigration and as to the treatment of the immigrant after he is admitted to this country.

It is true that the Congress of the United States has for several years devoted, and is now devoting, some time to the enactment of immigration legislation. But so far most of the legislation along these lines has been of an emergency character and has been added to the patchwork of immigration law which has grown up during the past century, enacted to meet varying conditions at various times. It is probable that the right solution of the problem of the alien on his way to America and in this country will be a matter of years so far as legislation is concerned. It is well, therefore, that every American should devote some thought to the problem which is vital to the country today and in the future. For immigration affects us not alone as a matter of economics and of political development, but as a direct and lasting effect on the life blood of America. To some extent the kind of Americans that will inhabit this country in the future depends upon the character of the immigrants we admit today, and upon the treatment accorded them after their arrival in this country.

PREFACE

There is a longing almost universal in our
alien population to become part and parcel of
this great Republic, to join in the life, language,
and customs of this country, and to devote
themselves to the perpetuation of American
ideals. It should be our purpose and responsibility to foster this desire; to make clear and
easy the way to true Americanism; and to see
to it that these people are given the opportunity to know America, to learn our language,
and to embrace our customs and our ideals.

It is with the full knowledge of the feelings
of our alien population that this book has
been prepared, and with the hope that it will
serve in some small degree to awaken a deeper
interest in the stranger within our gates.

In the preparation of this work a great deal
of material has been analyzed. It has been my
endeavor to make it as authoritative as possible.
I have sought and received the assistance of
men qualified by experience and training in
order that the material herein presented might
not express merely personal opinion, but, as
nearly as possible, fundamental truths. I am
deeply indebted for this assistance to Mr. A.
E. Hamilton of the Carnegie Institution of

PREFACE

Washington, at Cold Spring Harbor, Long Island, New York; the Assistant Secretaries of Labor, Hon. E. J. Henning and Hon. Robe Carl White; and my secretary, Mr. Arthur E. Cook.

JAMES J. DAVIS

WASHINGTON, D. C.

CONTENTS

CHAPTER   PAGE

    I The Immigration Policy of Egypt.........   11
   II Major Migrations   20
  III American Immigration Policies   27
   IV Our National Intellectual Stamina   35
    V Alien Feeble-Minded and Insane   43
   VI Criminalistic Aliens   59
  VII Bootlegging in Orientals   69
 VIII Dumping of Undesirable Immigrants   75
   IX The Cost of Poor Immigrant Stock   86
    X The Immigrant Trail in America   93
   XI Deportation   99
  XII Immigrant Groups in Our Cities   105
 XIII Immigrant Standards of Living   114
  XIV Assimilating Worth-While Aliens   126
   XV The Enrollment of Aliens   136
  XVI The Vital Index   144
 XVII Fecundity of Immigrant Stock   155
XVIII The Blood of Our Founders   161
  XIX Effects of the World War   168
   XX A Look Into the Future   174
  XXI Three Jewish Migrations   180
 XXII Distinguished Immigrants   187
XXIII Substantial Immigrants   197
 XXIV Conclusion   207

APPENDIX

    A Summary of Immigrant Legislation   217
    B Pertinent Facts   223
    C Increase of Population Due to Immigration   224
    D The Quota Laws   226

SELECTIVE IMMIGRATION

CHAPTER I

THE IMMIGRATION POLICY OF EGYPT

The history of the Egyptians is on record for us only about as far back as 3500 B. C., but from these records we may presume that the civilization of those people had its beginnings much further back in calendar time. Tombs, mummies, and skull-shapes, as interpreted by those whose lives are devoted to their study and significance, tell us that at the dawn of its history Egypt appeared as a land of homogeneous people, a distinct racial and political unit in the world.

So far there had been no invasion nor infiltration from foreign races. The old Egyptians passed an immigration law designed to keep the stock of their nation uncontaminated by the blood of the vast, unknown land to the southward. They built great forts on either side of the River Nile and wrote upon a rock the first hint of a policy of selective immigration. The rock said that the southern Africans might come into Egypt individually to visit or to trade, but no shipload might pass the forts down the river. A few, coming into Egypt to trade, could be watched, and, if they tended to become settlers, could be deported or summarily dealt with for breaking the spirit and the letter of the law. Wholesale immigration was prohibited, and the forts stood there to enforce the prohibition.

About 3000 B. C. saw the coming into Egypt of a strong and vigorous Asiatic element which filtered in gradually and made its impression upon the nature of the population and its culture. This slow influx was followed by a somewhat aggressive expansion of the Egyptian people, pushing their boundaries outward to the west and south. Art, architecture, and agriculture showed signs of a progressive mental stimulus. This immigration of sound, vigorous stock gave advantages which were of social, civic, and racial benefit to the Egyptians.

Fifteen hundred years later a sprinkling of weak kings gave the races to the south, the Libyans to the west, and the Hyksos to the northeast, a chance to gain a foothold on Egyptian land. These people were recognized as inferior but they were allowed to come in, and as a result civilization dragged. Finally open war arose between the Egyptians and the Hyksos, resulting in the expulsion of the latter and the militarization of a large portion of the Egyptian people.

With the adoption of warfare by a hitherto peaceful and agricultural people, came the practice of making slaves out of captives. Instead of expelling the foreigner, he was kept partly for servitude. This has always resulted in a final assimilation of the slave into the social and racial structure of the people. It has also meant the lowering of the standard of the stock by the admixture with another, and usually an inferior, strain of blood. Hybridization tends to reversion to the lower type. Only when two equally sound and able stocks mingle their blood is there a chance for stability or advancement.

Racial intermixture marked the beginning of the decline of Egypt as a great nation and a great people. Military victory, making slaves of captives, and imperialistic pushing out of borders together with pride in progress and civilization was followed by the importation from other lands of slave and servant labor.

Under Thothmes III, one of the greatest Egyptian kings, the blood of the nation was further watered and thinned by encouraging a slave-servant class to come in and serve the large and prosperous middle class, the clergy, and the king.

Along with the watering of the blood of the old Egyptian nation through intermarriage with the slaves of conquest and the imported serf labor of other, less civilized lands, there arose the dominating power of the clergy. Magic and mysticism replaced thought and invention. Egypt became one vast church, and its people a superstitious and servile congregation, worshipping sacred cows, bulls, alligators, and beetles. The lowered racial level of the people was reflected in a lowered level of thought. The dark ages of Egyptian history set in.

Periods of anarchy, followed by the assumption of power by strong men who temporarily got the country together and on its feet again, were followed by renewed control of affairs by the clergy, and by military dictatorships. The military regimes were characterized by the use of hireling soldiers and alien allies. Egypt depended upon foreign blood. The Libyans continued to ooze into the body of the nation from the west; the alien races to push up from the south. Egyptian kings married Hittite princesses from the Semite lands to the northeast. The blood of Egypt continued its mongrelization and its face turned backward to past glories instead of looking forward to things to be.

Slowly but surely foreign blood became dominant. In the year 945 B. C. the Libyans took an open and literal power and Egypt officially passed into the hands of a people who for generations had filtered in, almost unnoticed.

But the Libyans were not the strong race that the old Egyptians had been. They did not retain their power, but gave place to another foreign people, the Nubians, who, in turn, faced invasions from the always threatening northeast, first from the Syrians close by, later from the Persians from farther north. A country mongrelized in blood, divided in culture, submissive to the magical cycles of a mystical religion, could not long endure as a nation of itself.

Egyptian civilization, as exemplified in huge temples, magnificent but hardly used pyramids, luxurious courts, and a growingly prosperous clergy, throve on cheap labor, on the foundation of unskilled manual work of imported racial stocks.

If we look upon great pyramidal piles of rock, huge colonnades, stupendous monoliths, and a rapidly expanding foreign trade as marks of a nation's success, then Egypt was successful beyond the dreams of its old kings in the days when Egypt was sufficient unto itself. But history teaches us that a pyramid may endure, and a temple may stand, and Cleopatra's needle may adorn a Central Park thousands of years after a great people who produced these things through the labors of an inferior people has vanished from the earth.

The people of Egypt today are a mongrel race, a scrambling of an indefinite variety of widely differing peoples, an example of the tendency of all hybrids to revert to some primordial, primitive type. What the world owes to Egypt is a debt due the old, original, solid Egyptian people who built a civilization of their own before letting down the bars and allowing alien races and peoples to inherit what they themselves had built.

We have no records of Egyptian birth-rate at

the time of the great builder kings, in the days when the calendar was invented, when engineers discovered the principles of the arch and learned the balance of roof and column, and worked out stupendous projects of irrigation. It may be that the birth-rate among Egyptian men of science was as low as it is among American families of scientific men. It may have been that science and the religion of mysticism, which followed it, contributed a sterilizing influence to the upper levels of Egyptian stock. Or, this may not have been the case.

We can only judge the past, where we have no records, by comparison with the times in which records have been kept. Surely the history of ancient Egypt, especially in relation to its immigration from foreign lands, strangely parallels our own in many striking instances. Perhaps it paralleled it in its birth-rate. Perhaps there, too, the alien produced two children to the Egyptian's one, as our own foreign population gives two children to America for every one born to a native son. We cannot be sure, but we do know that Egypt fell into the hands of the stranger within her gates; and we do know what a swamping birth-rate will do!

It is not to be inferred that America's birthright is being sold for a mess of cheap-labor pottage and that the commonwealth of our forefathers, which should be the heritage of our children, is to belong to the children of alien races and people. But, for the welfare of America, today and tomorrow, it behooves us to consider carefully what sort of foreigner, what quality of alien, we are allowing to share in the civilization of this great Republic.

We need not build forts for the exclusion of any race, but we can erect a selective plan whereby only those individuals of any race may be admitted to America who are fit to become incorporated in our social and civic structure. In this way we can do much toward keeping the blood of the nation unpolluted by inferior strain. Almost every civilized race today is mongrel, in a sense, made of diverse racial elements, fused in the melting pot of time. Most civilized races contribute good, sound strains of family and individual; and also such races are spotted with defective, degenerate, and inferior lines and stocks. It is for us to consider seriously the problem of discrimination, of selection, of exceeding care as to whom we admit as future parents to America.

[18]

We will not tolerate any system of espionage registration of either our aliens or our nationals; but we can, by establishing a plan of enrollment of aliens, know where these aliens come from, where they go, and what kind of men and women they prove themselves to be, before they are admitted to citizenship, or return again to their native lands. Such an enrollment, with a re-enrollment annually, e. g. at the alien's local school house, will not only keep us in touch with him as a prospective citizen, but it will enable us to help him become a better citizen through those many agencies which we have built up in the interest of true Americanization.

This measure will not assure us a purity of racial stock entering America. Neither will it very markedly raise our immediate standard of living or of human quality. But we shall have made a beginning of a definitive policy, aiming to indefinitely postpone, if not entirely prevent, the weakening of our whole social and family structure as a nation by the introduction of jarringly discordant elements of difficult, assimilable quality.

CHAPTER II

MAJOR MIGRATIONS

Immigration in the past has struck our shores in waves—great waves of restless, desirous humanity, flooding in upon us all too often because of political or economical troubles at home, and with little or no reference to what the inflow might mean to America.

During and immediately following the War of the Revolution little attention was paid to even the most superficial aspects of immigration. In 1780 no sort of count was kept of people coming into America, but from 1784 to 1794 we have very reasonable estimates which would indicate that about four thousand persons came over annually. From 1790 to 1810 the average inflow was at the rate of approximately six thousand per year, with perhaps ten thousand coming over in such years as 1806 when England blockaded French ports, and France retaliating, declared English ports in a state of blockade.

In 1809 the United States prohibited commercial intercourse with Great Britain and France for one year. A year later Napoleon's decree was annulled, and we were able to resume trade with France, but at the risk of interference by Great Britain. Then came the War of 1812 with England which further restricted immigration to America very stringently.

After the Napoleonic Wars, the first great wave of immigration reached America in 1815. In that year two thousand men and women came from Brittany. In the year 1819 the number increased to thirty-five thousand. This influx of French Huguenots we might call one of the results of the downfall of Napoleon Bonaparte. These people were a sturdy, upstanding, independent stock. The few thousands who migrated to America made a splendid contribution to the blood of our nation.

Up until the close of the period above mentioned, there were no American laws regulating immigration nor having to do with shipping in relation to immigrants. Ships were small, unsanitary, unventilated, and always crowded. With the pressure of immigration, the crowded conditions grew worse until they became intolerable. Disease spread among the immigrants very quickly on the sea-voyage, and great numbers arrived in hospital condition.

On March 2, 1819, an act of Congress laid down certain regulations as to passage across the ocean, insisting on a specified minimum of air-space between decks for each passenger, demanding that food and water be adequate for the entire voyage, providing for proper ventilation, cleanliness of quarters, and limiting the numbers in accord with the tonnage of the vessel.

It was well that this was done, for immigration increased steadily from 1819 on up to the time of our Civil War. The following short table shows the rate of increase of alien arrivals only:

1819-1829	128,502
1829-1839	538,381
1839-1849	1,427,337
1849-1859	2,118,404

The Germans contributed to the second wave. Those who answered the call of William Penn and helped him found Philadelphia and other colonies in Pennsylvania, added greatly to the sterling qualities of our nation. The pioneering of these first German settlers inspired others, mostly of like caliber, to come across. Some sixty thousand arrived in Philadelphia before the Revolutionary War. The later German migration was caused by the revolutionary troubles in Germany of 1848 which stirred thousands to seek for peace in other lands. Among those who came to America were many political exiles, independent and liberty-loving, who contributed no little original and intelligent thought to our country's store. German peasants, hearing of free land, came also with traditions of hard work and with a fair degree of native intelligence.

A third great wave may be said to be the influx of the Scotch-Irish. About fifty years after our Revolutionary War, the Celts began migrating to America in numbers. Ireland was over-populated, and the people on the whole were poor. The more ambitious and energetic, hearing of America, broke home ties and came over to better their fortunes. This migration drew from the better stock or blood of Ireland and became an asset to the New Republic. On the whole, Ireland has made splendid contributions to the building of America. The Irish in the United States have brought us many sterling qualities and lent muscle and brain to the construction of our common-wealth.

Other migrations also came. The peaceful Swedish invasion began after the Civil War and culminated in 1882 with a landing of fifty thousand. Later began the great migrations from southern and eastern Europe— Italians, Slavs, Greeks, and later Armenians— at first a gentle ripple of twenty thousand on our shores in 1876, and rising steadily to three hundred thousand in 1907.

The three waves, the Huguenots, the Pennsylvania Germans, and the first influx of the Scotch-Irish brought us varying qualities; sensitivity and artistic talent with the Huguenots, industry and economic thrift with the Germans, and tough, fighting, hardfisted pioneer stuff in the Scotch-Irish, but all characterized by the underlying essential of good blood and sound heredity.

After our own troublous economic times of 1893, there was a halt in German immigration, and when the inflow was resumed, as our free land was all gone, the type of German immigrant stock changed. People who would endure the rougher work, the lower standard set by the general tide of industrial immigrant, "cheap labor," came over in place of the political exile and the homesteader.

The same difference in type is noticeable in the immigration from Great Britain. First sending us her Puritan pioneers to clear the forest and get a firm grip on the soil of America, she followed with generations of the settler type, the land-getters, the home-makers. When the land was practically gone, her artisans still came, and the better grades of her industrial workers.

Cheap labor from southern and eastern Europe brought down wage scales and standards of living. Labor that valued itself, labor that required a certain higher standard of living stayed at home rather than come to America to compete with slum-boarding-house conditions created by our impatient demand for quantity production at any cost. So the racial stocks represented in our immigration very definitely changed.

From this we must learn the wisdom of a definite, selective policy in immigration. We must have laws that will help raise the general average in the point of blood or stock. If we do not, there is danger of America's sliding into the hands of the descendants of poor human quality. Then the ideals of our founders would not have the ghost of a chance to remain dominant in the Republic. For, the lessons of poor heredity are written large in the history of peoples since written records began, and it is time we applied what little is applicable of our knowledge lest indeed "the weak shall inherit the earth."

CHAPTER III

AMERICAN IMMIGRATION POLICIES

The history of immigration in America shows three epoch-making attitudes toward the subject. These attitudes we may regard as forerunners of an immigration policy, a national conviction on the matter of who shall and who shall not be welcome to the United States as guest or as future citizen.

First came the idea of asylum. America was a land open to the oppressed, the freedom-seekers, the persecuted of all lands, and of all races and peoples. Any one could land wherever there was footing. Plymouth Rock, Manhattan Island, the James River, the Florida Coast, and the mouth of the Mississippi all beckoned to the newcomer without reserve, restriction, or question. The attitude of asylum, the idea that here was a refuge for all ills, was prevalent during the early years of our history.

Gradually the second, or economic attitude, came to the foreground. When the colonies had become a nation, and when problems of labor demand and supply became acute, this attitude toward immigration labor grew up slowly and naturally. In 1855 the people in the "Native American Movement", popularly known as the "Know Nothing Party", became alarmed at the coming of foreigners who had been accustomed to work for wages lower than those prevailing in the United States. They campaigned for restriction of immigration but finally their demands dwindled to the mere exclusion of paupers and criminals, and even brought out a reaction in favor of encouraging immigration.

The economic aspects of immigration steadily grew, and, with the hard times of 1892-96, this phase of the question became acute and overshadowed all other considerations. The Immigration Bills passed in 1903 and 1907 were restrictive, and raised the standards concerning undesirable citizens, but the principal motive behind all this legislation was economic, dealing with competition in labor, standards of living, and the importation of common labor from abroad.

This attitude culminated in the appointment

by President Roosevelt of the Immigration Commission authorized to make a complete survey and investigation of the whole immigration question. The findings of the Commission, in forty-one volumes, showed the necessity for a policy of restriction in accord with economic conditions in the United States. The study showed that too great an influx of aliens reduces the standard of living in America for the people as a whole, works hardship on American labor, and, in the long run, may prove disastrous from the standpoint of assimilation. It pointed clearly to the adoption of the percentage basis of limitation which was adopted only when the great tidal-wave of after-war immigration actually threatened to swamp the Republic with a flood of heterogeneous humanity of every conceivable variety.

The third, or biological attitude, that will prove fundamental to our future policy in immigration, was marked by a first-hand investigation into the quality of our alien and foreign-born stocks as reflected in our institutions for the socially unfit.

A Congressional Committee on Immigration and Naturalization wanted first hand facts as to the burden upon the American taxpayer, and upon American society, due to alien dependents. This committee, of which Representative Albert Johnson of Washington was chairman, had listened to scores of persons of various viewpoints on the immigration question. Those wishing to see our doors closed completely brought statistics in support of their claims. Those who wished our immigration to remain entirely free and open marshalled their statistics and arguments and brought them forth. Those who favored a happy medium did likewise. But in each viewpoint there was an element dealing with the inherent quality of the immigrant as a prospective member of an American community, and it was this element of quality, of immigrant stock or blood, that led the committee to appoint Dr. Harry H. Laughlin, of the Carnegie Institution of Washington, to conduct a thorough investigation of our alien and foreign-born with reference to their general stamina and quality.

The problem of investigating our fourteen million foreign-born men, women, and children, distributed in many centers of population, cannot be handled adequately. But the third of a million alien and foreign-born inmates of our state and federal institutions could be studied with very suggestive results. So Dr. Laughlin and a corps of investigators began to analyze the various types of social dependents in these institutions with reference to their place of birth, their nationality, and race, and the proportionate contribution of each race and nationality to the total custodial population.

Only state and federal institutions were studied, as one of the aims of this research was to estimate the cost to the tax-payer of maintaining our state and federal wards. Private and municipal institutions were left untouched, it being presumed that the study as limited would give us a good sample of the general state of affairs in all similar institutions.

The survey covered 445 state and federal institutions, including those for criminals, insane, feeble-minded, blind, epileptic, tubercular, deaf, and unclassified dependency. It included the statistics concerning 210,835 inmates, and its classifications and results have been considered representative and sufficiently typical to afford the basis not only for further study, but for some very definite conclusions with regard to the role immigration plays in burdening society with the unfit and socially inadequate.

This investigation covered such points as the proportion of foreign-born to native-born among the feeble-minded, the criminal, the insane, and the dependent. Suffice it here to say that the survey proved beyond all doubt that higher standards of immigration selection, and a more rigid administration of such standards, would do a great deal to lighten the burden upon society from the results of weak blood, poor human quality, and inferior types that otherwise have been sifting into the United States from foreign lands.

The conception of America as an asylum for the oppressed has been very much modified of late years. We have found that a great many of the oppressed in foreign lands were oppressed and persecuted because they were found unsocial and impossible citizens at home. We have found that advantage has been taken of America as a "city of refuge" by persons and even by governments seeking to rid themselves of undesirable citizens or neighbors.

Our shores have been dumping grounds for criminals, paupers, and anarchists. We have given the world an inch and it has taken a mile. America as an asylum for the religiously or politically persecuted lover of liberty has bid fair to become an asylum for the alien insane, defective, and degenerate. We have learned that the very principle of asylum must be safeguarded by the principle of selection of those who shall seek asylum here.

The conception of America as an unlimited field for the exploitation of cheap foreign labor has had to be modified. We have learned, almost too late, that cheap labor means a cheap people. We have learned that standards of living continually drop as we import more low standard persons than can be assimilated and adjusted to the American standard. We have learned that on economic grounds alone there is warranted such a restrictive, and, in a sense, selective basis for immigration as our percentage law has brought.

And, we are about to learn, for public consciousness is awakening to its significance, that the blood of a nation determines its history and that the kind of men and women we are admitting to America from other lands is going to determine largely what kind of country and what kind of history is to be ours in generations to come. As a corollary to this proposition, we are learning that the history of a nation may determine its blood; and that just in proportion as we guard our land against a peaceful conquest by men and women of a low quality type, will the ideals of our founders have a chance to live among us and among our children.

The third and latest attitude in the history of our immigration, then, seems to be by far the most important, and the adoption of a national policy of genuinely selective immigration for the benefit of our own and of all future generations seems so obvious and imperative as to call for immediate and intelligent action.

CHAPTER IV

OUR NATIONAL INTELLECTUAL STAMINA

Immigrant Americans are welcomed to the shores of a people who have made this a land where every man stands equal beside every other man before the law, and before the privileges and opportunities of American citizenship. Ours is a nation where there is no class distinction, where individual and civic worth will bring a man into his own, irrespective of where he was born.

And yet, in a country whose cornerstone is engraved with the legend that all men are created equal, and where there is no recognized aristocracy or serfdom, we find that certain individuals are born unequal to the responsibilities of citizenship and that there are among us some who are of very distinctly undesirable social material. These we have always had with us, but their practical problem and especially their relation to the future welfare of the United States has never stood out so clearly before. Our conviction that all men are created equal is sound democratic, foundation-stuff. Our antagonism to class distinction and discrimination has grown to be an organic part of our thinking and acting. Yet, there is a proviso and a modification to both these convictions.

Our great, composite American people are beginning to realize that we, like all races and peoples, are made up of two distinct classes; the socially fit and the socially unfit. This does not mean "society" or "blue-blood." It refers simply to bad and good stock, weak and strong blood. This is the only class distinction a free people should recognize. It is, translated into humanity, the same distinction that a farmer makes between crab apple and Baldwin, between good wheat and poor wheat, between sound cattle and scrubs.

To illustrate: An American soldier in the Revolutionary War had a son by a nameless, feeble-minded girl. Four hundred and eighty inviduals have descended from that mating in direct family line. Of these, 140 were distinctly feeble-minded, and only 46 are known to have been normal. Of the others, 36 were illegitimate, 33 notably immoral, 24 confirmed drunkards, 3 epileptics, 3 outright criminals, 8 kept houses of ill fame, and 82 died in infancy. This is what is meant by weak heredity, and the socially unfit.

The same American soldier of the Revolution married after the war and settled down. He married a wholesome, sound, normal woman. Their descendants have also been traced, counted, and classified. Out of 496 direct family descendants, only two have been known to be drunkards, only one notably immoral, none feeble-minded, insane, or criminal. The family tree is heavy with the fruit of honest, able, hard-working men and women, good citizens. Doctors, lawyers, judges, educators, writers, traders, landholders, and respected wage earners characterize this whole family. This is what is meant by the desirable class, the fit.

This family history, forked at its source and running down to the present day in two totally distinct strains—one weak, the other strong, one socially dangerous and a burden to the nation, the other socially helpful and a national asset—shows clearly that all men are not created equal.

The son or daughter of a feeble-minded man or woman is not the equal of the son or daughter of parents of normal mentality. No amount of training, opportunity, medical or surgical treatment has ever been able to alter defective heredity to a normal blood heritage. These facts are now proved beyond doubt. It remains for us to face them and to meet them with other facts, equally proved, which in time will enable us to greatly diminish the unfit strains from the blood of the nation.

If one American family has contributed so splendidly and also so unhappily to the sum total of our national intellectual stamina, we might wonder if there is any way in which one could judge or estimate the vigour of our national mind. There has been considerable debate and discussion in our newspapers and magazines concerning the results of our army intelligence tests as an index of the national intelligence. Some authorities conclude we are a nation of morons, or high-grade feeble-minded persons. Some are more generous and say we are a nation of adolescents, with minds of the average intelligence of a high-school boy or girl. Still others insist that the army intelligence tests as administered to a select group of our population are no indication of the average intelligence of America at all.

Very interesting facts have been discovered concerning the foreign population of our country, and concerning the kind of minds we are admitting to America from other lands. Carefully analyzed statistics show us that whereas our immigration law prohibits any feeble-minded person from coming into the United States, it is a fact that many do. Our expectation is zero, but the number of our alien feeble-minded in state institutions shows 32 per cent. That is, for every hundred inmates expected from the native white population of America, the foreign-born contribute thirty-two when, if our immigration law worked perfectly, they would contribute none.

Now, only a small fraction of our total feeble-minded population is segregated in our state institutions. It is estimated conservatively that there are some 450,000 definitely feeble-minded persons at large, and it is very probable that the same proportion of foreign to native born applies to them. Evidently, then, thousands of obviously weak-minded individuals have been admitted to our country who should have been kept out. For, our figures deal only with the lowest grades of mental inferiority; idiots, imbeciles, and morons.

What if we should set a higher standard of intelligence for admission to the United States? Suppose, for instance, we should take the lowest three grades of our army intelligence tests as a measure, or "passing mark." Suppose these tests had been adopted, applied, and administered so as to do their work perfectly. The three lowest grades of our army tests, called the C minus, the D, and the D minus, stand respectively for low-average, inferior, and very inferior intelligence. But even the lowest of these tests is higher than the average high-grade feeble-minded, or moron, could pass.

On the basis of the results of our army tests upon the white foreign-born men of our draft, it was found that six million of our present alien population of fourteen million would not have passed. That is, on the army-test basis, six million immigrants would have been refused admission to the United States. But doubtless such a test would not have been fair. While weeding out great numbers of the obviously deficient and defective, it would have turned away thousands of solid, wholesome, strong-brained, potential citizens.

Our army intelligence tests may be altogether too much a test of opportunity, and not of native potential ability. In a sense they partake of the nature of an intellectual stunt, and, probably, with practice, a very large number of those six million foreign-born who, it is estimated, could not pass the lower three tests, would manage them easily. Our immigration guards should be concerned with the native ability that grows sound, able, normal minds and not so much with the mere actual ability to pass a set of tests set suddenly before one. We need a higher standard of mental tests than we have at present, by which to judge the brain value of those who come to us from other lands. We need fair tests of mind-quality that will select for us a higher grade of mentality from all races or nationalities that would contribute to the building of our composite American mind, our national intellectual stamina.

It is to be desired that the Department of Labor, then, may contribute to the improvement of the mind of America as a whole; that it may put a stop to the inflow of inferior mental quality; that it may discriminate between lack of opportunity and bad or poor stock as the cause of mental inferiority. Here is a practical opportunity. Here are at least the beginnings of a fair and intelligent basis for selection of our immigrant population of the future, a population we hope to see rapidly assimilated and Americanized in the truest sense of that word.

What the Department of Labor and the Bureau of Immigration need, and what the American people need towards another step in safeguarding, preserving, and actually improving the quality of our national mind is a wholehearted public support of the principle of selection of immigration.

CHAPTER V

ALIEN FEEBLE-MINDED AND INSANE

The Bible tells us that the human race grew so wickedly degenerate at one time that God decided to start all over again and repopulate the world. He picked out a family of good old fashioned, God fearing, hard working stock and told it to get busy, build a ship, and save itself from destruction.

He also told the head of this family to pick out a first class specimen pair of each species of animals roaming in those parts and put them on board, too. The story does not mention plants, but we may credit Mrs. Noah's window boxes with what we have of floral beauty in the world.

And so the rains descended and the floods came and the wicked and degenerate race was drowned out and a new beginning was made. God wanted a world of better people, and this was the way, the story says, he got it. He selected the best and destroyed the others. That is the way Luther Burbank gets prize potatoes, monstrous berries, and splendid flowers.

We all want to see America a land of better people. We want less crime, less insanity, less loafing, less restless discontent, less weak-mindedness in our schools and on our streets. America is now the richest country in the world, moneywise. How about America's richness of national life? There is no real wealth but life. What is the measure of our wealth in happy, sound, wholesome, human living? We have no accurate standard as to that. Our national life is too vast, too varied, too complex to measure in such terms. But we have danger signals!

All history teaches us, as the President of one of our great Universities has so often and eloquently pointed out, that the blood of a nation determines its history, determines its growth and progress or its degeneration and its end. Let us therefore ask ourselves what sort of blood, what quality of stock is America producing; and, much more practically and measurably, what sort of qualities are we allowing other nations to pour into our national blood stream through immigrants and the descendants of immigrants.

Certainly the United States Immigration Service has done a great deal toward improving the quality of American life by keeping out degenerate types of mankind. With all its unavoidable leaks, with all the devious slipping in of feeble-minded, insane, potentially insane, criminals, and anarchists, our immigration law and its administration through our immigration officials has done splendidly in keeping out pollution from the stream of our national life.

Let us consider the one item of the feeble-minded. Theoretically, according to the letter of our law, the immigration service should keep out every feeble-minded person who comes to our ports. The law also provides that any who may slip in shall be sent back if they are found. But there are now, instead of no alien inmates in our state institutions for the feeble-minded, as should be expected, many thousands of these unfortunates. This shows us that our methods for applying the law against their admission must be improved if the law is to work with complete thoroughness.

Who are the feeble-minded? Definitely weak-minded persons are now classified in three distinct groups. Those whose mental age runs from zero to three years are called idiots. Those whose mental age is from three years to seven are known as imbeciles. Those of intelligence equal to children of seven to twelve are named morons. The term feeble-minded, herein used, covers all three of these cases.

Idiocy and imbecility are easily detectable. An idiot or an imbecile has little chance of slipping by our immigration authorities. It is the higher grades, the morons, that we must guard against most rigorously. The moron is the type defined by the British Royal College of Physicians as "capable of earning his living under favorable circumstances, but incapable, from mental defect existing from birth or from an early age, of competing on equal terms with his normal fellows, or of managing himself and his affairs with ordinary prudence." It is the type that can chop wood, lay stone walls, and tend chickens in our custodial institutions, where the cost of supervision almost equals the value of the work done, but, when loose on the street ends in the juvenile court, the reformatory or, all too often, in prison.

Morons, says an eminent American authority on mental defect, are often normal looking, frequently talk quite fluently, may even learn to read sufficiently to pass our present immigration literacy test, and, as children, may impress the average layman or even the average teacher as merely dull and backward. About 2 per cent of our public school children are feeble-minded, and the larger part of this number are morons. Perhaps improved methods of testing and investigation will show this percentage to be higher still.

The great decrease in immigration during the war enabled our examining officials to do their work more thoroughly. In 1914 some 2.6 per cent of immigrant arrivals were debarred, or deported within five years after landing. In 1916 the percentage was 6.1, showing a definite increase in the efficiency of our immigration staff when relieved of the time, space, and energy pressure of huge numbers. This suggests what the possibilities may be under a more intelligent immigration law and an abler and more complete corps of examining authorities than we have had thus far.

Vital to a more thorough selection of immigrants is a larger corps of men and women trained to spot physical and mental defects in the individual, and also trained and experienced investigators into family history. We want to know what sort of blood is being brought into America, as well as what kind of individuals comes in.

Figures tell us that we do fairly well in keeping out individuals of feeble mind. For each lot of 100 inmates of our state institutions contributed by our population as a whole, the same numerical lot of aliens contributes only 32. Bad stock, however, crops out strikingly in the second generation of our foreigners. Children of two foreign-born parents contribute 165 instead of an expected 100, and children of one parent foreign-born and one native-born contribute 190 instead of an expected 100.

A great deal of feeble-mindedness is hereditary. It behaves in what is called a "recessive" manner. It hides away over a generation, so to speak. While a feeble-minded person may have a child who appears in every way normal himself, he may be a bearer of the hereditary weakness and it is almost certain to crop out in his children.

The facts and figures laid before the Committee on Immigration and Naturalization of the House of Representatives lead straight to the conclusion that, with respect to feeble-mindedness, in some instances the present immigrant is himself very much better than the blood, or hereditary family stock that he brings with him. He is, on the surface, much better than his children are likely to be. He contributes personally, perhaps, a good citizen, but he contributes a burden of unfit types to the coming generations of America.

Is it not fully time that, in considering the problem of immigration, we take into account besides the elements of labor demand and supply, besides the tradition of the open door to the oppressed or the ambitious of other lands, and besides the personal fitness of the individual, the hereditary qualities which an individual brings to America?

This is a relatively new thought in our social and political and economic life. We can do nothing drastic, nothing hurriedly, very little in the immediate future. But we do know enough about this subject to greatly strengthen the hands of our immigration service to the end that we may much more effectively keep out more and more of those types of humanity which make America less like the country we want it to be. The blood of a nation determines its history. It helps determine our happiness and the happiness and welfare of our children and their children. Let us do what we can to purify the national stream of life, to dry up the sources of hereditary poisoning, and to keep America sound at the core.

The purpose of the United States Department of Labor is to foster, promote, and develop the welfare of the wage earners of the United States, to improve their working conditions, and to advance their opportunities for profitable employment. A reduction of the tax rate would seem to be one way of promoting and developing the welfare of the wage earners of our states. The average man and woman would consider his or her welfare promoted by any measure that would lessen the pressure on the weekly or monthly pay envelope for state or federal expenses. And the Department of Labor, through one of its branches, has the power and part of the machinery to bring this thing about.

Under the Department of Labor there functions the Bureau of Immigration, empowered by law to guard our gates from an inflow of dangerous or undesirable persons from other lands, and to rid our nation of certain undesirable or dangerous persons who may by some means slip by our guards. A clause in our immigration law provides for the deportation of aliens who become insane or public charges, under certain circumstances, before they have been in this country for five years.

In the Kings Park Hospital, on Long Island, there were, on a recent date just 5,319 insane patients. Of these, 2,434 were foreign-born, and of the foreign-born over 1,000 were still aliens. Only 61 cases in Kings Park Hospital, however, were at that time deportable under the provisions of the immigration law. The rest of the alien patients had either been here more than five years, or it was not possible to prove that they had become insane through causes existing prior to their landing in America. So, because our deportation provision did not work out thoroughly, we have in this one hospital alone a case of supporting a thousand or more patients at a dollar a day each, or some $365,000 a year. While Kings Hospital for the insane may not be typical of all our institutions as regards the number of deportable aliens, or the number that might have been deported, it serves to illustrate in a general way.

For the cost of two months' maintenance we could deport these cases. A few deportations of this magnitude would enable us to maintain a deportation service adequate to scour the country, the prisons, the institutions for feeble-minded, and our insane asylums and thus purge ourselves of a vast quantity of useless and costly human stock which has been inflicted upon us as a nation. This deportation work would be reflected in lower cost of institutional upkeep, and, in turn in a lowered tax rate. When you stop to think that our total state expense alone (not including municipal) for maintaining all of these custodial institutions is more than $75,000,000 a year, it begins to mean something to you personally. If you live in California, 15 per cent of your state tax money goes to custodial upkeep, if you live in Connecticut, 20 per cent goes this way, if in Illinois 23 per cent, in Kansas 24 per cent, in Massachusetts 30 per cent, and in New York 20 per cent. The average state expense for the upkeep of our homes for the socially inadequate is over 17 per cent of all the state expenditures.

Now, forgetting for a moment the item of deportation, which is far from being the best approach to our problem, let us consider some other facts of immigration. According to the census of 1910, the foreign-born population of the United States was 14.7 per cent of our total population. If that foreign stock were just as good as our native with reference to insanity, it should have contributed only 14.7 per cent of the population of our asylums. But it actually contributed 28.35 per cent.

Let us turn from considering the population as a whole and look at conditions in one state, New York, for example, because we have a careful report from the New York State Hospital Commission from which to take our facts. The frequency of insanity among the foreign population of New York State is nearly three times that of the frequency of insanity among those of native birth. The actual figure given is 2.9 times the frequency. The average number of years which these foreign-born insane spend in New York hospitals is nearly 10, or, speaking from the actual figures, 9.85 years.

Practically half the population of the greater hospitals are persons of foreign birth, and cost about $1.00 a day each to support.

This $1.00 a day for each foreign-born inmate of these hospitals, and the $1.00 a day that it costs to support the foreign-born feeble-minded, the epileptic, and other dependents in various institutions of the state, amounting to approximately $4,000,000 a year, has to come largely from the pay envelopes of wage-earners. Directly or indirectly it is the wage-earner who pays the taxes and foots this bill.

These are conservative figures. It costs more today than it did when these figures were compiled. Both the cost, and the numbers of our asylum inmates have increased steadily every year. But why, you may ask, has not the Bureau of Immigration seen to it that these alien insane, feeble-minded, and otherwise defective persons never entered our ports? Why should we face a problem of deportation when our law will not allow an insane person or one feeble-minded to enter the United States? Why should we have to bear either the cost of custodial care or of deportation of people who have no business among us?

Insanity, and especially potential, or latent, insanity, is much more difficult to spot than feeble-mindedness. Many more insane, and persons who become insane, get by our immigration guards than do other classes of defectives. A man who may soon be in one of our hospitals for the insane may, at the time of arriving in America, be sane mentally and strong physically. The most skilled examiner may be baffled at such cases when they come to him as individuals to be examined, without a carefully worked out analysis of the family stock from which the individual comes.

America is a land of high-pressure intensity of life. Our immigrants come from relatively slow-moving, traditionalized cities, towns, and villages, and drop into a maelstrom of humanity where little is permanent but change, where life is stimulating, dramatic, swift, and intense. Nervous systems must be strong to stand the strain of American life, especially its town and city life. The immigrant usually strikes the city first, and his brain and brawn are both taxed heavily to get his bearings and become adjusted to the new world of people and ideas. Weak minds, unstable nerves, brittle mental stuff crack and break under this pressure. From the certificates of fitness issued by public health physicians our immigration inspectors may believe they are passing in men and women of steel or malleable iron when they are really admitting cast-iron which will not stand the strain.

The average age of our immigrants when they land is about twenty-eight years. The average age of commitment to our hospitals for the insane is forty-one years. This leaves us a statistical margin of thirteen years, on the average, during which the break may come. The question then arises whether the mental cracking and the final breaking down is due to causes that arise after the immigrant has landed and tried to adjust himself to American life. Carefully gathered reports from our institutions show that this type of insanity is rare among our aliens. In the vast majority of cases their trouble is hereditary.

Our law says that if an immigrant becomes insane after having been in the United States less than five years, he may be deported unless it can be shown that he is insane from causes arising after his admission to the United States. But the expense and skill required to examine into such an immigrant's background and history, and to prove that the cause of his trouble lies prior to the time he came over, bring up serious and practical difficulties. The difficulties and expense in this regard are so great that deportation of any considerable number of our alien insane, while doubtless it would lighten our institutional burden to an extent that it might pay, is not the most practical economic solution of our problem. We must begin as soon as possible to dig back into the antecedents of our immigrants. We must begin to organize a corps of experts to pass upon the probabilities of insanity and other hereditary defects coming from those who come over to add to the numbers and quality of our American people.

It is not true that the science of heredity is yet fully on its feet, nor can even the most thoroughly trained expert be sure of himself in forecasting the future of a man's children by looking up at the man's family tree. But progress in knowledge is sufficient to make it possible to greatly strengthen our selective immigration service by adding a test of hereditary quality to our present requirements for admission. Our officials should pass on the standing of a prospective immigrant in his home community as to his character, his solidity as a citizen, and as to the probabilities, judged from his past performance, of his making an upstanding, hard-working, and loyal American citizen.

CHAPTER VI

CRIMINALISTIC ALIENS

Eighty-five thousand American citizens killed by poison, pistols, knives, or other deadly instruments in the past ten years here in the United States! Burglaries increased, during the same period, twelve hundred per cent! Our United States worse than any other civilized country when measured by crimes of violence! In one state's prison alone fourteen hundred inmates guilty of taking human life! These are not theories about crime and criminals, they are facts—facts gathered by the Special Commission on Law Enforcement of the American Bar Association in an attempt to answer the question as to what causes our periodic crime waves and our perpetually rising tide of outright, proved crime.

At the risk of seeming to magnify one of the many cogent reasons given for this rather melancholy state of things, let us consider one causal element, namely the alien element in our criminal population, and discuss it, not as the principal reason, but as a contributing reason, one that we can deal with practically, and with real hope of seeing results.

According to a careful survey made in 1922, and based on the census of 1910, the quota fulfilment of alien stocks in our prisons was practically the same as that of the whole population, or 98.5 per cent to an expected 100 per cent. But from parents, one native white, and one foreign-born, the number contributed to our state and federal custodial institutions for persons convicted of crime was 115 per cent instead of 100 per cent as would be expected from the population as a whole. Our immigration law provides that no criminal shall enter the United States. We find hundreds of alien criminals behind the bars of our prisons. Do we make criminals out of normal persons after they arrive in America? And what of the children born of one or both parents of foreign birth? Is there any special significance in the figures we have considered?

If these aliens in our prisons are typical criminals, if there is a distinct type of person who is or turns criminal, how did these persons get past our Public Health and immigration authorities, who, by law, are required to turn any such persons back? This question has led to the inquiry as to the type of mind our criminals possess, and varying answers have been found to this question. A corps of expert psychiatrists spent more than a year trying to find what the average mentality of the prisoners in Joliet penitentiary was. They reported that the intelligence of the average inmate of Joliet was equal to the average intelligence of the average enlisted man in our army of the World War.

A noted American psychologist, on the other hand, who has studied thousands of cases of feeble-mindedness and crime declares that, "the hereditary criminal passes out with the advent of feeble-mindedness into the problem. The criminal is not born; he is made. The so-called criminal type is merely a type of feeble-mindedness, a type misunderstood and mistreated, driven into criminality for which he is well fitted by nature. We have seen only the end product and failed to recognize the character of the raw material."

We seem, then, to be up against a wide divergence in opinion; but looking more closely at the facts, perhaps we shall get at the real meat of the problem. The Joliet investigation reports on average intelligence. The psychologist reports on intensively studied, specific cases of the feeble-minded criminal. There are both kinds, without a doubt, the intelligent criminal and the criminal from lack of brains, or of unbalanced brain. However, we may doubt if any large number of our criminal population is genuinely normal and sound of mind. All our facts seem to point in the other direction. And most of our facts seem to indicate that our criminal population is recruited from unsound hereditary stock, from the bad blood that flows in the veins of our nation.

If this holds true of our alien criminal, if it holds true of our foreigner who marries into our native white population and gives us, in their children, a much higher number of criminals than come from our wholly native stock, then the question comes back to immigration and Public Health Service examinations again. How can we keep out the human element that turns criminal, or that begets children who enter a life of crime?

Judge Harry Olson, Chief Justice of the Municipal Court of Chicago, is a man who looks beneath the surface of things. He knows, and he says that criminal law has no personal effect upon mental defectives. Direct law enforcement against this type of criminal offender simply does not work. Punishment does not teach it anything. Attempts at corrective education fail. This type simply has not the mental goods with which to respond either to correction, instruction, or punishment. Let us look at a few facts from Chicago.

There is a modern, thoroughly equipped, psychopathic laboratory connected with the Chicago Court. It is a laboratory designed for and equipped with a personnel to investigate the mental condition of persons who are brought to court through their anti-social conduct. This conduct may have been stealing a pair of cuff buttons from a five and ten cent store, or it may have been shooting a human being in the back. In either case it was antisocial and a case either for the reformatory or for the prison or for the home for defective minds. It is up to the psychopathic laboratory to give its opinion of the case. Out of 779 cases brought into the Boys' Court, 654 were found suffering from *dementia praecox*. Their brains were softening. Their minds were going through a process very similar to that which the minds of very old people go through when they drift into what we call "second childhood." The cells of their brains were beginning to disintegrate, to run down hill, to melt away. And the first cells to begin to fall to pieces are those which in some way as yet not fully known, have to do with our moral sense, our conscience, if you please, our feeling for right and wrong.

Boys or men suffering from *dementia praecox,* or precocious (premature) dementia, simply lack the machinery for distinguishing between right and wrong conduct. They are not responsible. Shooting a fellow mortal in the back means no more to one of these unfortunates than hitting him on the chest with a fist or calling him a liar. There is simply no use in punishing this type of person; there is no use in trying to show him where he is wrong. His ear may hear words but his mind does not respond to their meaning.

While the exact method of inheritance has not been worked out for this condition, or the causes that bring this condition about, there seems to be very little doubt but that in nearly every case this malady is definitely inherited. *Dementia praecox* is a condition very common in our alien insane, housed in our asylums. It is very common to the children of foreign parents in this country, and to children of one foreign parent and one native parent.

The crimes or anti-social acts of boys, or of men and women thus afflicted reflect back on our immigration law, and on our Public Health and immigration services at least in part. Inadequate immigration laws, inadequate facilities for keeping out degenerate types, lack of knowledge concerning what sort of stock our immigrants come from reflect in turn on crime in America. America stands blackest among all the nations in the world in respect to crimes of violence. Anything that will lighten this blackness should be upheld and encouraged. Could not our immigration laws and our Public Health and immigration services very definitely help in this regard?

When a man like Judge Olson says that life has become unsafe by reason of the *dementia praecox* and the psychopathic type being at large in society in ever increasing numbers, we may begin to look for causes. And when we find that one important contributing cause is the inflow of aliens into America, bringing us this kind of stock even if not so notably bringing us this type of individual immigrant, we may realize that there is at least one cause which we can handle directly.

If we can raise our standards for incoming immigrants, if we can have time, facilities, and trained personnel to make the kind of investigation that is necessary to discover danger signals in a person's constitution, or the constitution of his family and near relatives, then we can definitely lessen, and possibly in time completely check, the coming in of the degenerate, and of the bearer of degenerates. If we can maintain our percentage exclusion law and make it more stringently selective of better types of men, we have another means both for excluding the poor human element, and for giving our immigration authorities more time to make their selection of individuals more thorough.

We want to welcome foreigners like Mr. and Mrs. Domenico Zacchea, to whom President Harding wrote a letter of congratulation for the fine large family of well cared for, normal children growing up into all the possibilities of good citizenship. We want to keep out the kind of degenerate-brained woman who, after poisoning her husband, sent her son John to the Pontiac reformatory for robbery with a gun. That John had about the same kind of brain as his mother had is evident even to the laymen who will read this extract from one of his letters:

"I want to go away with you and wont be back till we were over there and come home in this trick and keep it to the world in coming away in this world and coming from your mother and come home from your vacation."

This boy was actually found, in the Chicago Court's laboratory to be sub-normal, a moron; but his crime was already committed, and his mother had committed murder. The time to have prevented this crime was before the stock this boy came from was allowed to land in the United States.

Whatever our technical basis for selection may be—and that is a matter for Congress to decide—it is very evident to all who have studied this subject thoroughly that crime in America can definitely be lowered through more stringent selective standards of immigration. The result will not be immediate or dramatic. The mills of heredity work slowly, through marriage, birth, and development; but they work persistently and definitely, improving or impairing the whole quality of a race or a nation. Our immigration service aided by the Public Health Service can merely do its own, not unimportant part in contributing to the raising of the quality of the nation's blood, and the years to come will justify the means we must adopt to this end.

CHAPTER VII

BOOTLEGGING IN ORIENTALS

Seventy-three Chinese stowaways were found on board a vessel in San Francisco Harbor by our immigration authorities. Their history will give you a sample of one of the multitude of tricks that are resorted to, in order to bring oriental labor into the United States against our immigration law.

It was found that these seventy-three stowaways had been, for years, members of the crews of various steamers running between our country and China. They would go back from San Francisco to Hongkong as seamen, and there they would refuse to sign up for the return trip. Legally they abandoned their calling as seamen, and a raw crew was recruited to take their places. But instead of staying ashore, they stowed away on the same ship, and as soon as it was ready to set out to sea, they came out from hiding, manned their places, and brought the ship to America. When they arrived at San Francisco, they hid away again, and the dummy crew was on deck and also ready for shore-leave under the provision of our sixty-day shore-leave law.

Once ashore, this dummy crew would vanish, simply melt away among the city streets, leaving not the slightest trace of itself. The regular crew of professional sailors on the ship would then come out of their hiding, take their posts, and return to China to go through this performance again and again, until they got caught.

The only means, perhaps, for combating this sort of practice effectively is through the registration of all arriving aliens or seamen. If these seventy-three Chinamen had been registered, and were required to show their registration cards, we would have a means of detecting them. Then our deportation law would do the rest.

Seamen, actual or bogus, members of legitimate crews or mere padding added to regular crews for the purpose of getting in, and all aliens actually landing openly in our ports, could be registered. But those who are smuggled past our borders in motor-trucks by night, those who are dropped upon us from aeroplanes, and those who dart into our lonely bays in motor boats from bootleg schooners beyond the three mile limit, are another problem.

Our immigration department, investigating conditions in Cuba, found that there were strong indications that from twenty thousand to thirty thousand Chinese coolies on that island were there for the sole purpose of getting smuggled into the United States. Thousands pay the heavy Canadian headtax of $500 to come in and settle themselves advantageously along our border until the time is opportune to slip through. Shiploads of coolies come through the Panama Canal to the British West Indies, not to settle there and work, but to lie low until the word comes that, for the payment of an average of $150 each, they can be sneaked into Florida or one of our Gulf States.

But a still more startling and daring venture has come to light. Evidently the great pressure for entrance to our country is well financed, and its results very profitable. For example: it was proposed to the Department of Labor that a large number of "industrial students" be allowed to come to the United States from China. Our immigration and exclusion law provides that bona fide Chinese students may come to America, and thousands of such students have come to our schools and colleges, proving welcome visitors and a credit to the land of their birth. But the term "industrial students," and the large number proposing to come under this name, looked suspicious and consequently a careful investigation was made. The long and short of the results of the inquiry was that a gang of immigrant-bootleggers had actually gone so far as to secure a concession for bringing some thirty thousand coolie laborers to the United States under the camouflage of collegians!

Doubtless these thirty thousand coolies would have obtained an American industrial education, and some of them even an agricultural education, but what the promoters were looking for was not the educational advancement of their students, but an estimated profit of about $3,000,000 on the deal! In fact the chances for this profit were so good that for months after the concession had been canceled, the coolie-procurers tried all sorts of methods to have the concession re-instated, and even to punish those who had a hand in preventing this preposterous trick.

Since 1892 the American people have been committed to the policy of excluding Chinese and other oriental labor. The exclusion acts have been changed from time to time to suit conditions that have arisen, but it is now time to carefully revise and amend our law on the basis of facts, and also to strengthen the machinery for the execution of the law.

The basis of a new law should be the registration of all Orientals now in the United States. To begin with, we need a special census and registration. Then we need a rigid registration of every Oriental arriving in America. Each one should be required to keep his registration card. Lacking this card, the person would be subject to inquiry as to when and how he came. If it were proved that he came in accord with the law, he could then be registered and given his credentials. If it were not proved, he would be subject to deportation. The law should be so framed, also, that it would exclude the laborer, but otherwise encourage commercial relations with China. It should favor the merchant, the bona fide student and the intelligent traveler seeking information.

Careful investigation shows that in the summer of 1921 there were some 2,500 stray seamen in New York City, from oriental countries. It would take $250,000 to deport these alone, and the appropriation for deportation of all kinds for that current year was only $250,000. What we want is less deportation, not more. We want to stop the inflow. We need a revised law, we need a strengthened arm of the law to administer it. Let us make our Oriental exclusion law really selective—selective of only those few Orientals who we know from experience are welcome here, and rigidly exclude all others.

CHAPTER VIII

DUMPING OF UNDESIRABLE IMMIGRANTS

You may believe in evolution, or you may not. You may believe in a literal interpretation of the Bible, or you may not; but, if you will read any good textbook of American history, and if you will read the wonderful story of Exodus in the Old Testament, you will believe in the survival of the fittest.

What happened in Palestine when the Children of Israel migrated from Egypt and struggled to settle down in the Promised Land? What became of the Moabites, the Amalekites, the Canaanites, and the Philistines? They made it hot for the followers of Moses and Joshua, to be sure. But so did the American Indians make it rough going for the pioneer founders of our United States. The fact is that the people who followed Moses in that great migration survived and founded a civilization. The people who followed Miles Standish and Captain John Smith survived, and founded a civilization. The various "ites" of the Promised

Land disappeared. The American Indian has become picturesque history.

Now, just a few words about the survival of the fittest among the American pioneers themselves. Let us glance back once more at some of the elements that went into the making of the backbone of the Republic. In the first place, it took from six to ten weeks to sail from Europe to America. The little ships were crowded tight, they were unsanitary, and there were no modern methods for detecting and handling disease. Rough weather, coarse food, mostly salt meat, fish, biscuits, and stale water, all tended to lower the vitality of the passengers. Epidemics broke out very frequently. Thousands of bodies, history tells us, were thrown overboard; bodies not strong enough to stand the strain of the voyage; bodies unable to resist the attacks of disease. The more resistant, the stronger, the more fit men and women survived to land on our shores.

Then began the struggle on land. We know what the winters were. Half the Mayflower Pilgrims died before that noble ship turned back to England. A fifth of the Puritans of 1629 died in their first year of battle with the wilderness. You recall the Indian massacres and the practical extermination of Jamestown. It took hardiness, strong bodily resistance and endurance, as well as moral and physical courage, to survive that struggle. On the whole, the fittest survived, and had children.

We all know well the history of the coming of great numbers of sturdy English, Dutch, French, German, Irish, Welsh, and later, Scandinavian pioneers, and of the early inhabiting of America by upstanding, virile stocks. But perhaps we are not so familiar with the manner in which human chaff got mixed with the wheat.

Preceding the Revolutionary War, the American Colonies were regarded as a fit dumping ground for undesirables, and even for criminals. Condemned criminals in England were even given their choice between coming over to American plantations or being hanged, and many of them preferred hanging! In 1717 the British Government deliberately organized the deportation of criminals from England and the landing of them on American shores. The Collector of the Port of London said about other undesirables at this time: "Most of those that go to America have no habitation, and are better out than within the kingdom." The famous Doctor Johnson even declared that the Americans as a race were little better than convicts and "ought to be content with anything we allow them short of hanging." Some fifty thousand convicts from England were dumped upon America before 1776, when our Revolution put a stop to this sort of "immigration."

Of course all these convicts were not necessarily bad stock. There may have been some political prisoners among them who added to our wealth of free, daring, independent men. "Give me liberty or give me death" were the words of a man whom the British government of that time would have hanged if he could have been caught.

But the fact remains that a lot of the weak-minded people who go wrong because they have not the backbone to go right, were landed here, dumped upon us long ago, and the results are with us still. It was the kind of stock that gave us families like the Nams. The Nam family is one of those traced back to days before our Revolutionary War. About the year 1760 there settled in the mountains of Western Massachusetts a family of vagabonds, part farmer, part hunter, and part fisher, who began to contribute their share to the population of America. It would not be fair to print their real name, as there are some few respectable citizens descended from this family source. So we shall call them the Nams.

Joe Nam had 8 children, and 5 of these migrated to New York. Their second generation numbered 13, the third, 29, the fourth, 70, the fifth, 194, the sixth, 397, the seventh, 146, and the eighth has thus far produced one, as a beginning. Seven hundred eighty-four members of this family have given us the following roll of social inferiority: 180 illegitimate children, 232 notably immoral women, 199 notably immoral men, 19 epileptics, 24 insane, 15 asylum orphans, and 40 in state prisons and jails. New York State has spent $89,000 in supporting, arresting, jailing, and custodially keeping members of this family. It has been conservatively estimated that its dead-loss cost to the community has been about $270,000.

This is merely one more sample of what happens under unrestricted immigration. It shows what we might avoid by raising our standards for the selection of our immigrants.

We cannot undo the past, but we can guard the future of America. We want no more dumping of undesirables upon us. We want no more settling in our Republic of vagabonds. We want to prevent such multiplication of unfit families in the future.

Selective immigration means merely setting our standards high enough to insure us sound minds and bodies from whatever race or people we admit as our guests, or as future citizens. We want to pick them out before they start across seas, if possible. We want to test them out for native quality, not for mere intelligence of the moment. A man may make a splendid citizen even though he can neither read nor write. He can never make a decent member of an American community unless he has sound native quality, good heredity, clean blood.

Our self-respecting, law-abiding immigrants and aliens themselves have time and time again protested, both through our English press and through their own language papers, against the weakness of our selective methods. As an example, Lieutenant Petrosino, writing for the Italian *Bolletino della Sera,* New York, says:

"The United States has become a refuge of all

the delinquents and bandits of Italy, Sicily, Sardinia, and Calabria. About a year ago the authorities of Tunis decided to cleanse the Italian quarter of that city where there were a great number of crimes. The French Government proceeded to make a rigorous inquest which resulted in the expulsion of ten thousand Italians from the country. Where did that flower of manhood go? They were welcomed with open arms by Uncle Sam!"

America, known to all the world as a land of refuge for the oppressed and persecuted peoples of other countries, seems to have become an asylum for bandits, black-handers, and land pirates. Murders, piracies, kidnappings, and blackmail have become so common as to be regarded as mere press copy for our evening newspapers. A chief of police of one of our largest cities remarked, concerning crime in one of his foreign quarters: "Oh, we've always had trouble up there; they never bother anyone but each other."

An incident was reported to the Congressional Committee on Immigration which illustrates an attitude in foreign countries that, since England began dumping her criminals and undesirables on our shores before the Revolution, has doubtless influenced for the worse our immigrant stream. The report reads:

"Some of our finest and most desirable immigrants come from Norway; yet a Norwegian judge, after sentencing a young offender to prison, was persuaded to allow some of his countrymen to send him to America instead! Thus our immigrant population was increased by one more undesirable, who would perhaps become the father of future American citizens."

We can hardly hold it against another nation that it would prefer to be relieved of caring for its undesirables if there were a safe and easy method of sending them away to some other country where they would find "asylum," either freely mingling among the people, or housed in a custodial institution. If our selective immigration sieve were fine enough, the fellow citizens of a criminal would think twice before raising a purse for him. They would find him returned to them, not only for safe-keeping, but minus the money spent to send him across seas.

Our great numbers of hard-working, ambitious Italians retain, in their community life, many solid virtues and wholesome traditions brought to America from the native soil. Their family life is shot through with affection, with loyalties, and with many sterling virtues. The best of them are not content with poor working conditions nor with poverty. They struggle up to high standards of living. They make good citizens. Time will make them a social and cultural as well as an economic asset to the Republic. But on their heels there follow the parasites, the knife carriers, the writers of skull-and-bones letters, the bad blood of the home country. From this we wish to see our selective immigration laws and authorities protect us.

Back in 1864, Abraham Lincoln favored a bill encouraging immigration to the United States. This bill was passed, but it was repealed in 1868 because it was found that our protest in 1866 against dumping undesirables upon us did not seem to carry sufficient weight. Switzerland and other countries were actually pardoning murderers and other criminals if they would emigrate to America! This practice has long since ceased, and there is no official dumping from other lands, but neither is there any very strenuous effort on the part of other countries to retain at home any undesirables who may wish to emigrate.

In 1888, a Congressional committee found that numbers of immigrants coming by steamer to Quebec would, within forty-eight hours of landing, apply for food and lodging in charitable organizations of New York State. Even today we have case after case of immigrants arriving at our ports, steering for the nearest organized charity and saying: "Here we are, what are you going to do for us?" Such is our reputation abroad for the care of our alien dependents.

Times now are good. We have no breadlines. Nearly everyone is at work, thanks in part to our breathing-spell in the matter of the foreign inflow of what once was surplus labor. Charity dumping is at low ebb. Criminal dumping in large quantities is practically impossible. Our immigration authorities have a lesser number of immigrants to inspect and to investigate, so the personal selection and sifting is finer. Under these conditions, it would seem that now is the very time to consider seriously and carefully the immigration policy of the American people; that now is the time to work out in detail an intelligent and inclusive selective basis on which to stand.

A great many measures have been presented to our Congress. There will be an infinite discussion of detail. But there is one big, vital issue. It is that we have a policy, laws, and machinery adopted that will make immigration selective of the better types of men and women, measured by higher standards of personality and of racial quality or stock. We want only sound individuals.

Whether we favor a further restriction of immigration, or whether we prefer a larger number of immigrants than our percentage now allows, at least we stand on the ground of a firmer basis for the selection of those who do come in to dwell among us.

CHAPTER IX

THE COST OF POOR IMMIGRANT STOCK

Let us take the arbitrary figure of 100 as a basis for comparison of the contributions of several races and nationalities to our prisons. Let 100 be the expected quota for each of the native-born races in the United States. Now let us set down in two columns a representative selection of peoples from northwestern Europe and southern and eastern Europe. The numbers opposite each represent the number of foreign-born persons contributed to our state and federal prisons for each expected 100 from our native population as a whole.

Switzerland	27	Austria-Hungaria	68
Ireland	31	Russia-Finland-Poland	126
Germany	35	Portugal	185
Great Britain	43	Italy	218
Netherlands	58	Turkey	240
France	125	Balkan States	275

Without regard to the individual immigrant, without regard to one's personal and family stock, our percentage law evidently, on this showing, would cut down the percentage of criminals of foreign blood in our prisons, for it lowers the percentage of races and peoples in the second column, who make the heaviest contribution to our prison population. And, as reflected in our prisons, so would the good results be reflected in our population as a whole, for by no means all our criminals are in jail.

The percentage basis works for the betterment of our population with regard to the incident of crime. But the percentage, or wholesale basis of admission is not enough to keep out dangerous individuals, individuals of contaminating heredity. For this purpose we have a system of personal inspection which, if improved and brought up to the level made possible by what we already know of methods of selection, would very notably cut down the influx of inferior types.

This second, or retail method of selection, is by far the fairest test of fitness, and were it not that we must protect our country from the great wholesale pressure of immigration which would completely swamp us with human material hard to assimilate and Americanize, it would be the better way of selecting our guests and future citizens.

It may easily be true that a great deal of

crime and disorder on the part of our foreigners is due to slow or faulty adjustment to our American customs and ideals. Immigrants from some countries of Europe undoubtedly find a wider difference between their way of life and ours than do immigrants from other European nations. Still the question of stock remains. Are differences of custom, tradition, and ideals, largely inborn, the outgrowth of the very human stuff that holds to them, or can they be changed by transplantation to a new environment? Will our "melting pot" do the trick? It will take years, perhaps generations, to answer this question, but meanwhile the immediate, pressing question of crime and criminals remains. We must take the benefit of the doubt to ourselves. We must protect our country in every way we know how from an influx of weak, unstable, defective, and deficient human material. This the Immigration Service can help to do if its hands are strengthened by law and if it is furnished the means to do its job thoroughly and well.

One way in which this can be done is by furnishing our immigration service with more trained experts in the detection of faulty mentality, the kind of mind that is easily shunted off into a life of crime. Another way is through a corps of trained field workers investigating and analyzing the history and reputation of our immigrants and of their families. This must be done in the countries from which they come. It is today a proposal not without its difficulties.

The point is, however, that with the tide of crime rising in America, reflected in constantly mounting figures, any practical measure for its reduction ought to be considered. Stopping the inflow of criminal types, or feeble or unstable-minded types who turn criminal, from without will not solve the problem but it will very definitely help to solve it. It will very surely cut it down and enable us to deal with the problem, as a whole, more effectively from within.

In 445 of our federal custodial institutions, including those for the insane, feeble-minded, epileptic, blind, deaf, tuberculous, and paupers, there is a population of some 210,835. The percentage of foreign-born in the population of the United States is 14.7. Using this percentage, there should have been some 25,366 foreign-born inmates in these institutions. Actually there were found 35,612. In terms of the expected contribution from native and foreign-born stocks on the basis of 100 for the population as a whole, the native-born contributed 93 and the foreign-born 140 to our institutional population.

This difference in rate is too high. It seems to reflect directly on the efficacy of our immigration law or upon the administration of that law. Aliens coming to America are, by law, supposed to be of the kind that will not become public charges. That they should so become within certain limits, or even up to the average of the native population might conceivably be excusable by force of circumstance, if we stretched our generosity to its limit; but that they should give us such a quota as 140 per cent instead of the 0 per cent technically to be expected, or 100 per cent as an extreme maximum seems beyond all reasonableness.

According to the last complete survey in 1916, our several states spent on the average 17.3 per cent of all their expenses on the upkeep of institutional dependents. The total state expenditures in 1916 for this purpose was $75,203,239. Doubtless today, with increased numbers in our institutions, and the higher cost of maintenance, this figure would reach $100,000,000.

At present some 20.63 per cent of our institutional population is foreign-born, so that on the average 3.57 per cent of our state expenditures for all purposes goes for maintaining aliens or foreign-born persons in these institutions for the dependent. If we include persons with one or both parents foreign-born in our estimate, calling this "foreign stock," we find the percentage raised to 7.63 of state expenditure, chargeable in large measure to weak foreign blood in the veins of our nation. The report to the Congressional Committee says:

"The present cash outlay for maintaining social inadequates is only one of the relatively minor costs of degeneracy. We found in several types of the inadequates that the children of immigrants fulfilled their quota to an extent several times greater than that fulfilled by their immigrant parents. Here the responsibility of the Federal Government is to exclude inadequates and potential inadequates.

"The law, of course, attempts to do this, but our institutional survey shows that the law needs strengthening, and that the immigration service needs greater support and means for enforcing the provisions of the statute.

"If the Federal Government had to maintain all of

these inadequates at its own expense, there would be more poetic justice in the whole situation. As the matter stands, the Federal Government has the authority in relation to immigration, whereas the several State Governments have the responsibility and expense of caring for dependent immigrants and their children, who have slipped into the United States through the federal sieve.

"The Federal Government attempts to ease the situation by deporting certain inadequates, but the statute of limitations is so short—five years—after which immigrants can be deported, that this last line of defense is not, when measured in the light of national economics and race conservation, an effective remedy."

We have here a very direct appeal from the States to our Federal Government for facilities for better selection of our immigrants. The cost of aliens to our several states in social inadequacy requiring institutional care is certainly great enough to affect the pocketbook of every taxpayer. Three per cent or 7 per cent of total state expenditure means 3 or 7 per cent of each taxpayer's contributions to the support of the state. If, through more thoroughly selective measures, our immigration service can in a just and practicable way, lighten this burden, does it not deserve universal support?

CHAPTER X

THE IMMIGRANT TRAIL IN AMERICA

"By" Corey would hang a cow-bell around his neck, steal a neighbor's chicken and, swinging it around his head on a string, run up and down the street yelling "I'm crazy, I'm crazy!" Ben Yak lives alone in a roadside shanty and growls like a bear at school children passing his door. Maggie Chad has outlived two husbands and lives with a third, to whom her former husband sold her for a shot-gun. Mrs. Glade is so lazy she will not wash her children's clothes, even when these are given to them, and they run naked in summer in order to have a bit of clothing for winter wear. Rob Jincade and his pals filled up a sixteen-year old boy on corn whiskey, thought he was dead when he lost consciousness, took him out in a field and buried him. A farmer saw them and dug up the lad, took him to a doctor and he was brought back to consciousness.

These items are not clippings picked from a newspaper and put together. They are a few samples taken from a lot more like them from one single American community whose folks are all so inter-related by marriage that it is practically one large family, sprawling over a considerable ravine and valley territory in the Northwest.

The late superintendent of the school for the feeble-minded in the state in question wondered where so many defective children came from, and sent his research assistant to find out. She struck this gulch country, which she has called the Vale of Siddem and made an exhaustive study of its inter-tangled family trees.

The dwellers in the Vale of Siddem are known to their neighbors as low-grade farmers, timber rats, herb-doctors, and bark-eaters. The ravine where most of them live is variously known as Dry Run, Hog Hollow, and Hell Hole. To get an idea of what the research assistant was up against in tracing family histories, study the following sample:

"But the record of Doble, son of Jake, out Herods Herod in the sum of abject degeneracy among his descendants. Doble married Deborah who bore him one daughter. Deborah's daughter lived with her half-brother, Dick, who was one of Doble's eight children by a second wife. The illegitimate daughter of Deborah's daughter lived with her father's brother and bore him one child. Deborah left Doble and married Vide. But the daughter of Deborah and Vide married the feeble-minded son of Doble and his second wife."

The original settlers of Hog Hollow were migrants from the State of New York. In New York they had fraudulently settled on Indian lands, had been driven off by the state authorities and had wandered westward, leaving a trail of defective children in their wake. Finally they settled in this remote gulch in the West.

Sixteen hundred individuals have been charted of the families in this hollow, some of whom have spilled over into other parts of the state. They have contributed 256 mental defectives, including the feeble-minded, insane, and epileptics; 125 have been openly, flagrantly immoral; 15 have been out and out criminals; and 134 have been classified as alcoholics. An alcoholic in this sense means a person habitually under the influence of liquor. And besides this, in pauperism, sickness, consumption, and general shiftlessness, the "bark-eaters" have proved themselves on the whole a heavy liability upon the normal, hard-working people of their state.

The stock of the dwellers in the Vale of Siddem seems to be Anglo-Saxon on the whole, although one woman of the tribe married a full-blooded Indian and bore him seventeen children. Since feeble minds and unstable nerves characterize these people so markedly, generation after generation, it is reasonable to suppose that their remoter ancestors were among those undesirables whom England dumped upon our shores before Revolutionary times. Somehow, at least, they came to America, were admitted among the original settlers and began their work of burdening society with ever multiplying bad stock. Their trail is traced from New York to the Northwest. Pressure of population forces some of them from their ravine nest every little while, and the poor blood spreads out.

Our institutions for the feeble-minded increase in numbers and in size every year. Appropriations grow larger and larger. Taxes go up and up for the support of our burden of inadequates. Meanwhile immigrants come streaming in from Europe, bringing us splendid qualities and sound heredity in some; bringing us just the kind of human stuff that peopled the Valley of Siddem, in others.

It will probably be a long time before we can accurately predict the caliber of mind a child will have from a study of his parent's family history. Family records are not kept fully. An investigator usually finds it hard to climb very far up into a family tree, or even out onto many branches where reliable information grows. The true science of heredity lies in the future. But enough is known now to warrant going ahead with these studies. Enough is known now so that it becomes a practical question as to whether we shall add field workers in heredity to the staff of our Public Health and immigration services.

Insanity, feeble-mindedness, epilepsy, and general constitutional and psychopathic inferiority do run in families. Families characterized by these defects can be spotted and tabulated. One member of one of these families, coming to America and begetting children, may cause us to spend more money on their care and on the protection of society from their antisocial acts than the money it would take to provide field investigators for every port of immigrant embarkation in Europe.

It is too early yet for us to know what effect our recent immigration has had or will have on our American stock as a whole. Field workers cannot make such studies as the one just referred to among families of immigrants of one generation or even two. Family history spreads out fan shaped from an evil source, and weak-mindedness, insanity, constitutional inferiority crop out here and there in single spots or in bunches, as the family grows and spreads. But we have enough examples of what does happen to predict what may and probably will happen. We have sufficient knowledge to keep us alive and awake to the possibilities that lie in admitting inferior people to America. We must strengthen the hands of those who keep guard at our gates. We must utterly stop the stream of the weak and the degenerate that trickles into our country from abroad to lower the average stamina and mentality of our nation.

CHAPTER XI

DEPORTATION

Suppose you had been seasick for four or seven days on your way across the ocean in the crowded steerage of a throbbing steamship. Suppose you had then landed on a little island off the coast of a strange, mysterious land whose language you did not speak, whose customs you did not know, and where you had but a few friends, or none at all. Suppose you had spent your last cent to get across the ocean and knew you had to make good on shore or starve. Suppose you knew that before you got ashore you had to run the gauntlet of uniformed clerks, police, attendants, guards, doctors, and psychologists. Suppose you knew that if you did not stack up to a certain physical and mental and moral standard, you would be sent back across the sea on the next boat.

What sort of a frame of mind, what sort of a mental machine would you have when it was your turn to sit down before a little table, look into the boring eyes of a formidable psychologist, and pass an examination designed to test your mind-power in a score of different ways? Would you behave in the same way, mentally, as you might if this same psychologist had come to your house in your own home town over-seas and placed before you his curious set of tests and begun to ply you with questions? Or even if you had come to your port of departure in your homeland, and had been faced there with the same examination, would not your state of mind, your whole mental make-up, intellectual, and emotional, have been quite different, and much to your advantage?

And so it would be with our immigrants, greatly to their advantage to pass their tests of fitness to come to America before they started the long sea-voyage. Some day we hope to see our investigators, examiners, physicians, and psychologists translated from our ports of entry to the various points of departure of our prospective immigrants. It would not only enable these officers to do their duty more thoroughly and more efficiently, but it would give the immigrant a fairer deal. While we should have more time and greater facilities for discovering defects and dangers, he would have ampler opportunities for proving that he was of the kind that would be welcome in America.

This would also relieve our immigration service of much of the harshness and at times of the genuine cruelty of deportation. Our immigration authorities are not hard-hearted despots, eager to send back men, women, and children who do not quickly stack up to our technical requirements of admission. They are human beings, bound in duty to execute the law requirements of admission, irrespective of personal feeling in the case.

When a person is definitely found to be criminal, prostitute, feeble-minded, epileptic, insane, or obviously bound to become a public charge, he should be deported at once. But the grounds for deportation are varied and sometimes involve untold hardships on the deported, and upon their relatives and friends besides—hardships that could have been avoided had our selective work been done at the point of departure instead of at the port of arrival.

Our present percentage basis for admittance to America has relieved the general immigration situation materially. It has given us a breathing spell and a better chance to assimilate our foreign-born from sheer point of numbers, but it needs much supplementing in detail. It does not directly affect the deportation problem, which remains much as before.

Under the quota limit acts of 1921 and 1922 the Republic of Liberia was allowed to send to America 3 per cent, yearly, of the number of naturalized Liberians in the United States. Under this law the Mayor of Monrovia, Liberia, reached our shores just too late to be included in his country's quota. Statistics showed that during July only one half of a person could be admitted from Liberia, making half the Mayor eligible and half not eligible to come in. The case was held up to be passed upon, and, as no provision had been made in the law for human fractions, and as the Mayor was obviously a desirable guest, it was passed favorably upon the recommendation that this gentleman from Liberia be admitted. This instance is merely illustrative of the fact that the percentage laws do not respect persons, are not selective of individuals, and work hardships on the good, the indifferent, and the undesirable alike.

This resulted in steamship companies racing

to dock their ships in order that their immigrant passengers might be the first to pass in under the quota scheme. Ships waited outside the three mile limit until the instant a new month opened and then dashed for port to discharge their human cargo. This is all very natural under the law, but these facts tend to take our attention away from the real issue, which is one of genuinely selective measures of immigrant inspection, examination, and enrollment.

By enrollment is meant the practical banding together of our foreign-born for their mutual advancement along lines of Americanization and final assimilation as citizens, in letter and in spirit. This does not mean anything bordering or compulsory, or forced Americanization, but merely another step toward bringing the best elements in America quickly to our immigrant aliens that they may feel at home and begin at once to absorb the finest opportunities which this country holds, and holds in such abundance for everyone who has the desire and the capacity to absorb them.

One detailed phase of the enrollment scheme would include making provision for the dependents of any alien who might come under

the provisions of our deportation law, a law
which must do its work in certain cases, irrespective of the feelings of the individual, and
which sometimes must work great hardship on
persons not themselves affected by the law, but
dependent on those who come under its provision. Thus enrollment would be a mutual-aid
plan on a large scale, and would aim to bring
a number of very definite benefits to the aliens
themselves. It would naturally reduce the deportation problem.

CHAPTER XII

IMMIGRANT GROUPS IN OUR CITIES

Back in 1623 an immigrant coming to America was met by a reception committee of bears, hostile Indians, pathless virginal forests, and the mystery of the great unknown. He left his home town, or village, or city, and hit nature in the raw. The change was complete. Adjustment called for a thorough revolution in the immigrant's mode of life. If he had the nerve, the physical strength, and the power of will, he won out. If not, the environment got him, in its way.

Now an immigrant coming to America is met by a reception committee of folks talking his own language, people anxious to get his money, or to get a commission for selling his labor value, or to get his future voting power. He is led to a city block where, except for the height and ugliness of the buildings, he might just as well be back in the native town or village or city from which he came. The grocer, the doctor, the apothecary, and the minister all talk his language, as do the people. They dress somewhat differently, but the shop windows show him how this difference may quickly disappear.

If our immigrant today is from Italy, for instance, and lands in New York, he will find himself very much at home in a large Italian city bounded on the north by East Houston Street, on the east by the Bowery, on the south by Canal Street, and on the west by both sides of Mulberry Street. If he comes from Naples, Italy, he will find Neapolitans almost monopolizing both sides of Mulberry Street from Canal to Kenmore and sliding off east into Broome Street. If he comes from Calabria, he will discover himself practically back in his native haunts when he strikes Mott Street between Grand and Broome.

And so it goes. Our present day immigrants gravitate to large city groupings where people, customs, traditions, tabus, religions, and language, perpetuate themselves seemingly unchanged. Of course we know there is a slow but constant change going on, despite appearances. The work of the melting pot is sometimes and in some places exceedingly slow. But it is in the possible assimilation and ultimate Americanization of these immigrant groups that we are interested.

There has been, there now is, and there probably will be even more as time goes on, considerable intermarriage of various races and peoples in America. In the course of centuries this may mean the evolution of a new, composite type which generations of the future will distinguish as the new American type on this continent. Just what this type will be, no one knows. We have no way of prophesying scientifically, and the best we can do is to guess. But guesses into the future do not get us anywhere. Theories are beside the point. What is there, then, in the intermingling of our national and racial groups that counts for anything really practical with us today?

Just one point here as to the effect of racial grouping, as in our large cities, upon intermarriage, and upon the possible results, in the long run, upon our population. Facts show us that the larger the group of one nationality or race living together in one locality, the less is the probability of intermarriage with another race or nationality. Large groups tend to be sufficient unto themselves in marriage, and family relations, even if not in language and customs. This means that, provided the group is large enough, and provided it is made up of families of good stock, it will grow and spread out through pressure of numbers and contribute its own peculiar qualities to our population as a whole. If the stock is poor, on the average, and this inbreeding within the group goes on, the standards of life in the group, in personality, fitness, and character will drop lower and lower, and our population as a whole will suffer in proportion. Our standards of immigration must be such as to protect the very immigrant groups to whom new numbers come, and in protecting these groups from dilution by poor blood, we shall in turn be protecting our American people as a whole.

All down through the bituminous mining country of West Virginia, Virginia, Alabama, Arkansas, and Oklahoma, there are tight little colonies of foreigners in almost every city, just as there are much larger colonies throughout the cities of the Middle Atlantic and New England States. Fall River, Lowell, Manchester, Providence, Paterson, Jersey City, New Britain, Meriden, and hundreds of other cities have foreign colonies which are well marked and compact. In fact we may say that in every one of our large cities, the foreign colony is a fact, and with this fact goes that of inbreeding, of perpetuating racial qualities in children, for better or for worse.

With this picture in mind, then, let us remember that weak stocks intermingling tend on the whole to run down hill; and that strong stocks tend to keep up the general tone and level of the population. In terms of American life selective immigration can do its bit to render the contribution of our city-grouped aliens a better grade by adding to these groups new material of a higher order than has been in the past, or that would be of a higher order in the future without a more careful selection.

It has already been stated that our new immigrant steps from his steamship into a community practically like the one which he left in the old world. In a sense this is true, but in another sense it is not true. In one way, the inner revolution which our immigrant of today must go through in adjusting himself to his new environment, is almost as great as that which our first settlers had to go through.

The adjustment to American life means nervous strain. It means a heavy tax on all one's physical and mental stamina. It is a testing process, sometimes quite extreme; it is a trial by fire of the kind of human material that is newly come to the Republic. Here quality counts. Here good stock stands up under the strain. Here weak heredity leads to cracking under the stress and pressure of our highly organized, driving life. Here good blood tells in the capacity to take on new habits and to replace old ones, to adjust to a new community, to recognize new laws and customs, and to become, in a sense, a new person. Here, in high-pressure America, the man or family of weak stocks demoralizes.

For the Bureau of Immigration authorities and Public Health examiners there are only two types of immigrants, the sound and the unsound. If a man of apparently the sound type has gone wrong in his own country, and tries to come and join an American group of his race or nationality bringing with him sick doctrines, anarchism, criminalism, he is classed with the unsound. If

he cannot read or write, but in his home town
or village or community he has led an honest,
hard-working life and has the respect of his
fellows, he should be welcome. We can teach
a man or woman to read and write in America.
We cannot change a man's fundamental character.

So long as our foreign communities are made
up of men and women who are strong physically and mentally, we can trust our public
schools, our language, our customs and traditions to gradually permeate and leaven the
whole lump. It will take time; it will look perhaps impossible; but we must believe in healthy
human nature, in men and women who are
willing to work, who have the capacity to work,
the mental stamina to adjust themselves to
American traditions and then uphold and defend them.

Of course, some of our foreign groups in
our cities and in our rural communities are dead
set against assimilation or Americanization. So
long as it is honest and above-board and springs
from patriotic pride in their own nationality,
this opposition can do no lasting harm. It will
be worn down as American ideals and tradi-

tions prove themselves fit to play their part in the lives of these people. So long as the individuals of these groups are sound-minded, healthy, resilient, and plastic, we need have no fear as to the outcome. American ideals fit such folks, and will win.

Low ideals in morals or education come from a low grade of man. They usually come from a weak grade of man. Have you ever known a communist who was a well man, or a mere theorist who was not dyspeptic or otherwise ill? The ideas and ideals of the founders of our nation can never be undermined by the ideas that ooze out of sick men's brains. America is not going to take the slime of communism or the caustic of anarchism seriously. America is too healthy for that. But in looking back over the history of nations we cannot help seeing how sickly ideas have gripped whole peoples when they have become weak in the blood of the nation. We must hope that America will awaken to the fact that a nation's mind can be poisoned as soon as a nation's body is allowed to get soft. And the only biological way for a nation's body to become weak is for it to cease breeding from good stock and begin letting the poor multiply and inherit the land.

We must have an immigration service that will select those who come among us on the basis of native quality, of native potential to become good Americans. Let them come and join any honest nationalistic or racial group whose cards are on the table and who abide by our laws and respect our people. Let them hold to those customs, traditions, and ideals which have helped make them sturdy citizens of their native countries, and trust that in time, their being in America, their learning our language and our history, and their absorbing of our best traditions and ideals, will make them want to become a working part of this great Republic.

CHAPTER XIII

IMMIGRANT STANDARDS OF LIVING

The people of olden time, so the Bible tells us, took to heart the story of the flood and of Noah and his family. They got together and decided that they would become as wicked and degenerate as the people before Noah's day if they wanted to, and that they would put one over on the Lord if he tried flooding the earth again. So, the story runs, they built an immense tower whose top was to pierce the clouds, like the Woolworth Building on a day when the clouds are floating low; and in this tower they intended to hide and be safe if the windows of heaven should open again at the touch of the wrath of God. But the tower was never finished because these people were a mixed people and did not understand themselves. The builders did not understand each other's language. They talked in alien tongues one with another, and failed to do team work. And so the tower was called Babel, meaning confusion; work stopped, the people's dream vanished, and they went about their several ways without a common purpose.

Back in the year 1644 there were eighteen languages spoken in New York City, then a picturesque little country town. There were some ready in that day to talk in terms of the Tower of Babel about New York. But, while many of these native languages survived, practically everyone in the city talked English in 1775.

In Gibraltar, in Singapore, and in Hong Kong there is a welter of miscellaneous humanity, a confusion of tongues and peoples utterly bewildering to a visiting stranger. But there is no common purpose, no governing principle of nationalization, no concerted attempt or need for a common language. Each sectional people is sufficient unto itself, unto its small ambitions and its little dreams.

Today New York City has a larger Italian population than Rome, the capital of Italy. It has a larger Jewish population than did Jerusalem in the days of Solomon and his glory. It is composite of foreign colonies each one larger than most cities of the land from which it came. But the history of Babel is reversed, and out of chaos and confusion, there is coming unity of purpose and a splendid dream.

Yet here, to America, we have not only welcomed the individual immigrant family, but we find whole foreign colonies, foreign towns lifted bodily from old Europe and set down amongst us. Some blocks in our large cities are, to all practical purposes, foreign territory, with an alien language, a foreign-language doctor, minister, grocer, and undertaker. There are villages and towns in our Middle West clustered around a foreign-language school where English is taught about as French or Latin is taught in our schools, as a piece of intellectual embroidery.

The teachers of the children of our foreign-born in these closed settlements are often imported from abroad, are already growing old in the traditions and methods of their native country. While they sometimes bring customs and learning that may be of value to the young, they are opposed to the new. They cling to the intellectual and moral standards of their own youth, and they stand directly in the way of American-born children learning the American language and fitting themselves for life as it is lived in the United States. On the other hand, some people are in such a hurry to make American citizens of our immigrants that they would have them promise to do so as a part of the requirement for admission into this country.

But a Frenchman, an Italian, a Russian, or an Armenian is a patriot. He loves his country. He may come to America with the intention of remaining, or of returning home; of becoming an American or of remaining a citizen of his own country. If he is the kind we want over here as an American citizen, it is up to us to welcome him to the kind of country, the kind of people, the kind of privileges and opportunities that will make him want to become one of us. We do not want the kind of people that will lightly, and for an immediate advantage, promise to forsake their native country and embrace allegiance to another. After they have lived with us, absorbed our history, grown into our customs, learned our language, and come to love our country and our democracy, then let them of their own free will become citizens and Americans at heart as well as in name.

Americanization by intermarriage of races within our national melting pot is a slow process. What the typical American will be like a thousand years from now we have no means of knowing. Heredity, selection, and variation are the three mysterious powers of nature that make racial types work slowly and count their centuries as we do our days. But there is an Americanization by common language, ideas, and ideals that works much faster and is a much more practical matter for us to consider.

This Americanization through common language and understanding, however, is closely related to the kind of people to whom our language, customs, and ideals is put up. We cannot make good citizens of the weak-minded, of the constitutionally inferior, of the neuropathic by heredity. Again we strike the problem of human breeding.

We want to Americanize those who are quick to appreciate the opportunities and privileges of American life. It takes a clear eye and a keen mind to realize what these possibilities are. It is easy for the boobs, the dubs, the dumb-bells, as our school-boys call them, to see nothing but oppression, graft, pull, and "capitalistic tyranny" in the United States. What is the use of teaching English to anyone whose mental power is so weak he cannot see America as it is?

So, let us admit to this Republic only men and women with mental capacity equal to the ever growing opportunities for a life of real effort and solid work. Let us keep our selective standards high enough to keep out not only the actual imbecile, insane, and obviously incompetent, but also those weak, unstable minds that are such easy prey to our plague of reformers, hankering to shape America to fit their own weaknesses.

We want the kind of immigrants who have, in such large numbers, come to us in the past, ready to work, ready to learn English, ready to give a lot in return for the lot they get by giving. The way to have this kind of men and women with us, to build America, is to select them before they start for our shores.

Somewhere the Bible tells us that God looks not on the outward appearance of a man, but upon his heart. In passing judgment upon our immigrants and their standards of living, we must try to look behind and below the surface of things and try to discover what sort of mind is growing there.

A Polish professor gave up a good position in income in his home city because he could not teach in the way he wanted to. He came to America and worked at a dollar and a half a day, learning English while he worked and living, necessarily, at a dollar and a half a day standard. Hundreds of foreign students in the United States are washing dishes, driving carts, running elevators, and doing what we call menial work while they forge slowly ahead over the obstacles of a new and strange language, adjust themselves to new customs and traditions, and try to get their bearings right in a country as different from their own as the subway differs from a stage-coach.

On the other hand, it is largely true, as someone remarked, that immigration in the decade prior to the World War increased the number of hands, but not the number of heads, in the United States. Our Immigration Commission was forced to conclude that thousands of our immigrants are definitely below our average American mentality, and that there is very little hope of their ever attaining it. These are the people who are "watering the nation's blood."

Canada is a land that welcomes immigrants. Men are needed keenly on Canadian farms. The Canadian Parliament takes measures to promote immigration and holds out attractive inducements to the right sort of man and woman to come and settle. But Canada has discovered that it must watch its border, and immigrants whom we have admitted to the United States have been turned away from our neighbor to the north as being unfit for admission to the Dominion!

People, unlike water, tend to flow uphill. They flow from countries of a low economic level to those of a higher level. Cheap labor in the United States is considered well-paid labor in the lands where this labor comes from. Two dollars a day looks very small to a workman in a plant in Detroit, but very large to a hired farm-hand in Europe.

What accounts, then, for the tendency of certain persons in the land of high wages to migrate to Canada where wages, on the whole, are lower? Is there a contradiction here? No, we are merely brought back again to the question of human quality, of personal and hereditary stamina, of good or bad blood. Thousands of emigrants have been welcomed from the United States into Canada. The great Northwest is drawing heavily upon our best pioneer-settler stocks. Why, then, should we find some of our own immigrants, persons we have accepted as fit for Americanization, refused entrance into a neighbor nation?

We can only infer that it is because our standards of admission are lower, or that our methods of examination are not adequate, or both. Canada does not want to welcome persons whose standard of life is lower than the average for the Dominion, and one's standard of life is usually pretty well reflected in one's personal appearance, behavior, and general mentality.

Appearance, behavior, and mentality are largely the product of biological heredity. A person of sound heredity, of energy and native ability will not remain long in America and become the kind of person who is turned down when seeking admission to another land. There may be, and doubtless are exceptions, and the best of men sometimes slip and fall and go down; but talking in terms of average quality against the background of our general immigration experience, sound, strong stock comes up to average or stays above and forges ahead.

There is one point to remember in this matter of standards of living, and that is that our lowest classes, economically speaking, those of our people in the United States with the lowest standards of living, are still on a higher economic level than the average of the peoples from whom they are recruited. Our lowest average wage-scale, for example, looks mighty good to people in certain countries of Europe where actual starvation is no uncommon thing, especially in winter.

We tend, therefore, to attract a constantly lower living-level to America, and will continue to attract until the saturation point is reached and the levels balance. This would happen actually if we left immigration unrestricted and, however much we might raise our average level of living-standard, the lowering process would go on indefinitely as long as immigration continued.

Some day, what now seems apparent will be proved beyond doubt, namely, that the lowest economic orders of humanity represent, on the whole and in the average, the lower orders of native intelligence, of family or hereditary mentality. It is this question which our immigration law and authorities must meet and deal with as the principal problem in a policy of genuinely selective immigration service.

In any great foreign-city group you will find three characteristic mental attitudes. You will find people, mostly the old-timers, who cling tenaciously to old-world customs, traditions, and language. You will find people who are hard at work trying to adjust themselves to America as they find it, wanting to become Americans in spirit and in truth. And, you will find people who sit around telling each other what a sink of iniquity America is, and how much better it would be if they could re-shape it according to their heart's desire; a paradise without police, law, or work.

Sometimes the pressure of our American city life, the unexpected and sudden strain and stress on mind and nerve is too much for an otherwise sound and potentially able man or woman. Sometimes a good piece of human metal, with only a slight flaw, cracks and breaks as though it were weak and brittle. High-speed, high-pressure, urban life is sometimes to blame for the spoiling of otherwise good material. But usually, and on the whole, it is the natively poor, the unsound, the organically weak make-up, that gravitates to the third class, that gives us our social undesirables.

CHAPTER XIV

ASSIMILATING WORTH-WHILE ALIENS

Our immigrants may walk the streets of our cities for years, and hold aloof from America. They may live a long time in our rural communities and remain aliens in thought and speech. But if they are of the right caliber and continue to dwell in America, and especially if their children grow up here, America gets them. They become a part of its mighty growth. Without necessarily losing their own native individualities, yet they come to feel and to know what America is. The words of an immigrant himself reveal this process:

"America look like a blessed country, and I think I am going to great city, to grand country, to better world, and my heart develop big admiration, and a great noble sentiment for America and the Americano. I arrive in New York. You think I find here my idea? I go about the street to find the great history, to feel the great emotion for all that is noble in America. I do not see how the people can think to compare the American city with the beauty of Rome or Venice or Naples. I do not find much monuments to the great deeds, to the great heroes, and the great artists. I was deeply surprised not to find the fountains. I do not find the great art to compare with the art of Italy. But one day I see very, very big building. My mind is struck . . . . I have never seen anything like that! I say, 'There is the thing American, it is a giant.' "

It was the "thing American, the giant" that finally struck this young man's mind and became the starting point of his conception of what America means. But that was not all. That was but a beginning. Later on this same young immigrant found that America was a country of education for opportunity, both outside and inside of its schools. Of our schools, as he found them, he says:

"When I go to night school I had a good impression to me. The teacher treat everyone just the same. The Jew just the same as the Chinaman and the Chinaman just the same as the Italian. This was a wonderful impression. I went to this school just because I like the principal. He give it to me welcome like I was an American. I learn little English, and about the American Government, and how the people can make change and progress by legislation without the force of revolution, and I like very much this idea."

The public night school, the greatest of American institutions of assimilation and of Americanization, won a friend for itself. But it took more than great buildings and kindly teachers and a sense of fairness and justice and opportunity to make an American out of this foreigner of good blood, of native intelligence, and of sound loyalty to his own native land. The Americanization of good stock from other lands is slow. It has to be shown. It wants to test America first, before accepting it.

It was proposed to this young immigrant that, since he liked America and its schools and ways, he become an American.

"But I do not become an American yet," he says, "because I think always of the grandeur of the Italy civilization of the past!"

His home traditions, his country's history, his pride of nationality still stood in the way. Later on he married and, in his own words, as reported in the Red Cross Magazine, he tells us:

"I have not think about the future before, I have think about the past. Maybe I have a son. It is the future that is for him. America is to be his country. Why to live always in memory of past

grandeur? They were only men. I am a man and
my son will be a man. Why not live to be somebody
ourselves, in a nation more great than any nation
before? I see that big work to build the future.
I see the necessity to learn English, to become the
citizen, to take part in the political life, to work
to create the better understanding between the races
that they come to love each other, to work for better
conditions in industry, for health and safety and
prosperity—and it become more pleasure to work
than to take leisure. Suddenly it looks to me like
that is the American. It come to me, like I am born
—I am an American."

That is the type of man and mind we want
to see coming into the United States. That is
the kind we want our immigration authorities
to be able to select and welcome. We want
to see that type of potential citizen protected
from the other kind, the reverse, who comes to
America and blackens the name of the country
from which they both come. We must get together and work toward the future citizenship and blood of the Republic by lessening
the inflow of the slacker type, the type pre-
ferring leisure to honest work, revolution to
gradual growth and advancement. Higher
standards for selective immigration will help
us do this. Let us have them!

Our percentage basis for the limitation of immigration is thought to provide for time in which immigrants may become assimilated and naturalized. The capital argument that carried across the percentage idea was that we were suffering from national indigestion, and that a limitation of our immigrant supply would enable our body politic to assimilate and distribute its alien population. The provision does this, without doubt, but there are other factors than merely time at work. These forces, working very directly against assimilation and naturalization, we must meet on their own ground. We cannot afford to leave this matter to chance and time.

The war has created a stronger nationalism than ever in Europe. Man-power is again at a high premium. With millions killed and other millions incapacitated, the greater nations of Europe are tending to adopt definite policies to safeguard their man and woman power as nationals. Emigration is not to be left to chance. It is to be used for the benefit of the emigrant nation.

We were troubled, in war-time, by hyphenates. This variety of humanity does not simply grow, it is deliberately manufactured. It was a surprise to some of the old European nations to find that its supposed nationals did not flock back from America to the fatherlands as soon as the call to arms sounded. It was a shock to old Europe to find how largely its emigrant peoples had become assimilated into the structure of the New Republic. It was a lesson to those nations in the art of keeping their nationals loyal to the homeland.

The lesson has taught them that they must watch their emigrants from the time they depart; that they must extend them aid and protection after they land in another country; that they must make them feel that they are constantly under the protection of the power of their native land. The lesson carried home the necessity for lending economic aid, financial assistance, credit and opportunities for business progress, as well as mere paternal guidance and protection. Branch banks of the homeland, consular business service, the encouragement of investment at home, or the profitable use of home capital abroad are a few of the items in the new outlook, now crystallizing into a program. Emigrant nations have learned that they must strengthen the bonds between them and the native-language press in the lands where their nationals settle. They must work more thoroughly through schools and churches to keep the fires of home-land patriotism burning.

In the United States we see already signs of backfires set against this process. But too often they are the backfires of racial prejudice, national antagonisms, group hatreds, religious intolerance, and business jealousies. Too often, also, the remedies proposed are those of com-pulsion and legislation. There is a conception abroad that by passing new laws we can change a foreign national into a hundred per cent American. There is a spreading belief that all aliens should be required to become American citizens whether they want to or not. In these respects law and legislation become expressions of popular impatience, rather than of intelligent popular desire to see the making of good Americans who have become such from an inner desire and a solid pride in the fact. Schools, churches, social agencies, newspapers, magazines, lectures, business enterprises, and the whole, indefinitely varied pressure of ten thousand minor factors are working toward assimilation and final solidarity.

Without a doubt, the higher the type of immigrant we welcome to America, the more worth-while is his assimilation. And the higher the type, the harder the process will be from one angle and the easier from another. The alien who comes to us with a caliber of mind and an energy of body that will respond to the best things in America, is the type of man or woman who will find the readiest response on the part of America. He will find himself the most welcome, and the first to feel that he is being taken in and made a part of the whole.

But this type of alien will also be the kind who has the higher development of loyalty to his native land, who will find it hardest to break old ties, and to take on a new citizenship. Yet, how much better to take our chance on persuading such a man or woman of the value and privilege of American citizenship, harder though the process be, than to go after the other type whose naturalization and vote can be bought cheaply by organized political machinery. The mere fact of becoming a citizen and casting a vote is not what counts. What matters is the quality of man or woman who naturalizes and goes to the polling place.

The very type of immigrant whom we want to see become a citizen first is the very kind that will most quickly resent any attempts to force citizenship upon him, or to put him up against anything savoring of a legal require- ment to change his national loyalty. We want that type to become American, in spirit and in letter; but we want the whole man, willing and whole-hearted, and proud to be one of us. We cannot get this by law or by force. Citizen- ship is a matter, not of the head alone, but of heart and soul. We can get it only by convic- tion from within.

And the right type of mind does and will respond to the better things in American life. If we provide ourselves with the machinery for selecting higher types of immigrants, we will find it easier and quicker, on the whole, to make them a part of us than it is to as- similate the other kind.

In fact the lower types never can and never will respond to the higher levels of American life and culture. We know that education has to have material that can be educated to work with. We know that minds are like diamonds and pebbles; some we can cut and polish into gems, the others we can only use as best we may for whatever humbler purpose they may fit. And we have enough of the pebble material in our nation now, without importing more. Its birth-rate is much higher than the diamond variety. There will be no dearth of human pebbles for many generations. We want to see America attracting the best from abroad, and then taking such good care of it after it is here that it will want to stay, and give us the best that it brings.

Selective immigration will not solve the problem of nationalism nor assimilation; but it will greatly help. Through examination abroad, through an enrollment system over here, and by a constant pressure of kindly persuasion and sympathetic interest, based on our own loyalty and pride in the Republic, true assimilation will go on apace and help build up in reality the dream of all true Americans for the future of America.

CHAPTER XV

THE ENROLLMENT OF ALIENS

Ever since the Lord spake unto Moses in the wilderness of Sinai, in the tabernacle of the congregation, on the first day of the second month, in the second year after they were come out of the land of Egypt, it has been a practice of nearly all peoples to enroll their members in some form of census. The more advanced nations of Europe have very complete records of births and deaths, thorough census data, and many statistics of great human value which we totally lack when we wish to study the characteristics of our people as a whole.

Our own national census has been followed up by a registration of births. It is a symptom of backwardness in respect to our national bookkeeping that birth-registration is not universal for all our states. The area grows yearly, but we are still far from a national unit in this important item of national registry.

Tyrants have sometimes abused certain systems of registration, turning them into adjuncts of espionage and using them for purposes of unfair taxation. For this reason, some people oppose a measure for the enrollment of our alien population designed wholly and heartily for their own good and based on sound democratic principles of justice and liberty.

An enrollment measure has been proposed which will immediately begin to help all those aliens who come under its provision to become better friends of America. It will definitely lead them to understand the best which America has to offer; it will make them better and more quickly understood by the people among whom they have come to live; and it will lead to a larger percentage of naturalization in our foreign population than we have ever had before.

First, it will eliminate the present naturalization law requirement for witnesses who have known the alien for five years. A great many foreigners do not become citizens because they cannot produce such witnesses, or because the obtaining of such would prove too costly. It is estimated that the enrollment plan would save our aliens between three and seven million dollars yearly in the process of naturalization. By enrolling, and paying a small fee, the alien starts upon a course of educational Americanization and, in a sense, of insurance. Every cent of the fees collected should go directly to the purpose of making it easier for an alien to become an American citizen when he shall be eligible, if he then so desires.

Another provision of the enrollment fee should be, as has been suggested, the care of the alien who becomes destitute. Under present immigration laws, an alien who becomes a public charge, for whatever reason, before he has resided in this country for five years, is subject to arrest and deportation. Think of the tragedy which must follow when the breadwinner of a family of wife and children leaves them without means of support, either through accident, illness, or death. Deportation for those thus left destitute is a complete calamity, for they may easily have lost all touch with friends and relatives in their home across the sea, and thus our act of deporting them assumes the tone of unmitigated cruelty.

One of the provisions of this bill creates a fund, from the enrollment fee, from which this family could be taken care of and the children educated. This may seem paternalistic, but when the alien population is banded together under the enrollment system, much as a fraternal order is organized for mutual help, that stigma is removed and it takes on the essential elements of some of our leading fraternities.

Upon enrollment the alien will be given a card upon which will be recorded periodically his progress toward citizenship. If he is not desirous of becoming a citizen, the record will at least show what progress he has made in becoming a more intelligent member of his community, such as in learning the English language, in advancement along his chosen line of work. This card will be of use to him as an authentic identification wherever he may be, and whenever such identification may be found necessary or convenient.

The enrollment card will be a tie between the alien and the government which has welcomed him as a possible prospective citizen, and is desirous of helping him toward this end. It will in no sense be part of an espionage system, such as some aliens have been accustomed to in their native lands, where their very lying down and getting up is watched by a vigilant police. There has been some cry of objection to the enrollment plan by those who have misunderstood it, and compared it to European systems of espionage, totally distorting its meaning and significance and fundamental purpose.

True, an enrollment system would make it easier to detect and deport such bootlegged aliens or nondescripts who elude our immigration officials and break our laws; it would enable us to spot alien seamen who, taking advantage of the seamen's privilege of shore-leave, desert their boats and remain in this country in defiance of the law; but this is a mere by-product of a plan to make the path to citizenship, and intelligent citizenship, easier for the immigrant from abroad.

The contemplated new citizenship legislation is essentially a program of education in which every alien enrolls for training in citizenship. First comes the learning of English. Every alien will be encouraged to learn our native language as quickly as possible, both for his own economic and social good, and for the making of a more intelligent and useful member of his community. By no means does this imply that he should set aside or neglect his own language; but merely that, as a first step toward understanding America and being able to adjust himself to her conditions and profit by her privileges, a working knowledge of English is essential.

Other subjects may follow, such as history, civics, and political economy. Citizenship classes in the evening, with motion pictures and interesting lectures on these subjects will redeem them from any suspicion of dryness. They should be subjects of livest possible interest, and they can be made such very generally, as they are now in particular instances.

Through night school, public school, church, social settlement, foreign-press, and native-press, through books and lectures and the growing educational power of the "movie," lessons of real value can be brought home constantly to the stranger within our gates.

Periodically, perhaps at the school house, or at group headquarters, the alien may call to present his card with a record of his progress in brief, that this record may be transferred to the duplicate kept by the government. At the end of his period of probation, now five years, his record would show his eligibility for citizenship, and without further cost or the trouble of witnesses he would be welcomed in as a full member of his State and Nation.

We can picture to ourselves a great army of the foreign-born banded together through the enrollment system as one great fraternal organization working toward the fostering of better citizenship. Church, fraternal, educational, dramatic, and other civic organizations could play their part in helping the alien to feel himself belonging to this army of potential citizens and to take genuine and intelligent pride in his membership.

We can picture a recognized citizenship-day when a host of our foreign-born could be welcomed into membership in the Republic with a ceremony and celebration befitting such a step and such an achievement. We have initiatory ceremonies for new members of a fraternal order; ceremonies for admittance to church membership; special ceremonies for entering the state of marriage. Why should joining the American nation as a citizen be a mere matter of legal routine, left to the individual, a judge, notary, and a few witnesses?

The enrollment plan, with its corollaries in education for intelligent citizenship should lead right up to an occasion of momentous importance to every foreign-born guest of the United States. It should culminate in a recognition of a person's new status, befitting the privileges and responsibilities of his new role in life.

CHAPTER XVI

THE VITAL INDEX

When a mining engineer is asked for a report on a silver mining property, he first takes samples from the mine as it stands. He breaks off pieces of ore here and there as his experience and training direct him, has them assayed, and strikes an average ore-value for the mine as a whole.

When a scientist and statistician is asked to give us an estimate of the relative birth-rates in our foreign and in our native-born population, he has to go about his job in much the same way. Where there are figures available, he has to make sure that these figures are founded on fact, brought together by reliable people, and free from as many sources of possible error as can reasonably be expected.

Professor Raymond Pearl of Johns Hopkins University, has made a very complete analysis of our population from the standpoint of the birth-rate of our native and foreign-born inhabitants. His study is highly statistical, partly mathematical, and set down largely in charts and tables. But it is so significant that the gist of it should be known by everyone interested in immigration, and who reads this book.

Let us take a few samples from the body of facts gathered so carefully over a period of years of hard work. First, we find that for every ten marriages actually resulting in children, where the parents were of the same racial stock, there was one marriage of a native American with a foreigner. Like tends to mate with like. Our native Americans on the whole, tend to marry native Americans. Our foreigners tend to marry within their own race. The process of assimilation is slow, but it is going on all the time. The melting pot is at work.

The following figures are only a few, as samples, from the very complete set of facts gathered by this expert:

Marriages

America x America	816,546 or	65.0 per cent
Italy x Italy	76,251 or	6.0 per cent
Italy x America	12,559 or	1.0 per cent
Austria x Austria	46,407 or	4.0 per cent
Austria x America	9,600 or	0.8 per cent
Russia x Russia	53,128 or	4.0 per cent
Russia x America	10,519 or	0.8 per cent

There are seventy-eight such combinations in the study, and the outstanding fact is that 65 per cent of the children born in our area of birth-registration were from American-born parents. Of the remaining 35 per cent about 10 per cent were from one native and one foreign-born parent, and 25 per cent from the foreign-born.

Now what of the proportion of births to our native-born and to our foreign-born mothers? Again we have no accurate statistics, as our national bookkeeping of American life is sadly inadequate. We must rely on samples to suggest what is going on. During one year, in New York State, outside of New York City, there were 102,834 children born to white parents. Of these 64,889 were born to native-white mothers, and 37,945 to foreign-born-white mothers.

It is, however, the number of births per thousand of the total population that gives us the proportion in which we are interested. The number of births per thousand of the population given to this State by native-white mothers was 17, while the number per thousand given by the foreign-born-white mothers was

44. A careful review of the best facts and figures available, however, shows us that this proportion is somewhat too high to be characteristic of the whole population. Yet, we are safe in concluding that foreign-born mothers in America contribute slightly over twice as many children to the nation, per thousand of population, as do the native-white mothers.

From this very fact we may conclude that our immigrant population, while reproducing itself twice as fast as our native stock before it becomes assimiliated, attains the level of the native-white population when it has become a part of it. For our present native-white stock was once immigrant, either shortly or long ago. However, the net contribution of our foreign-born, so long as we admit immigrants, will, other things equal, continue to be proportionately higher than that of our assimilated Americans.

But that is not the whole story. The "Vital Index" of a people is not merely the birth-rate, but the difference between the birth-rate and the death-rate. Speaking broadly our foreign population produces two babies for every death. Our native population produces only one baby per death. Statistically it produces a fraction of a baby more than one, so that the vital birth-rate is not quite static, or stationary.

In our New England States and New York the native population is not reproducing itself. Vermont is barely doing so. Rural New York breaks about even between births and deaths. But the foreign population, especially in our great city groups, is vital in births over deaths and is multiplying rapidly.

In all forms of life it is the net balance between births and deaths that determines the outcome in the struggle for existence. Just as surely as our native stock does not reproduce itself, does not outbalance deaths with births —and our foreign population does outbalance death with life—just so surely will the latter survive and the former perish from the earth.

So much for these few suggestive facts concerning our population. We hope to see our standards of immigration so raised that if America is some day to belong to the descendants of our present and future immigrants, at least it may belong to those of good, sound hereditary qualities. There is no use lamenting the passing of a certain type and its replacement by another if the thing is done. There is every reason for improving a type if we can do it. Selective immigration is one way, at least, in which we can keep up, and even raise, the type of men and women who are to give us the American children of tomorrow.

A man with mental stigmatism and a reverence for big quantity and large numbers said:

"But if it weren't for immigration we'd be a little nation of a few million people. What could we have done in the World War if we hadn't had a huge population to draw an army from? Our native American stock is hardly reproducing itself. We've got to recruit our numbers from abroad in order to grow in man-power!"

It is not quite true that our native-born population is not reproducing itself. It is doing a little better than barely reproducing itself; but the foreign-born element of our people is producing twice as many children, and reproducing itself almost twice as fast as the native stock. There are, roughly speaking, two babies of foreign-born parents to every one of native-born; and the death-rate is about equal for both. It is true that immigration has brought millions of men and women to America. But it is not necessarily true that immigration has added to our total population as compared with what it might now be had there never been any immigration.

Thirty years after the War of the Revolution, there were about four million people in the United States. In 1820 there were ten million. The population had increased 150 per cent during a period when there was practically no immigration to America, owing to the British-French wars and our War of 1812. At this rate of increase of the native population alone, without immigration, we should have had a population of eighty million in 1895, whereas in 1900 our census showed only seventy-six million. Of course this estimate is based on the native birth-rate as it was. Benjamin Franklin put it at about six children to a marriage. Most families of the better sort had six or more children, and families of eight and ten were not at all exceptional.

Now our native families are smaller, and the remarkable thing about our national birth-rate is that the native-stock birth-rate has declined just about in proportion as immigration has

increased. Roughly speaking, in proportion as
we have welcomed those from abroad, our native stock has diminished its rate of reproduc-
tion.

Professor Pearl has shown that in those parts
of our country where a relatively large proportion of the population is foreign-born, the fer-
tility of the foreign-born women is greatly in
excess of the native-born. Almost the first
result of Americanization is to reduce the fer-
tility of marriages. Why? There are many
reasons, but one is that of the standard of living. When a native American family faces
the choice between reducing their standard of
living to that brought in by members of the
foreign invasion, and reducing the number of
children in the family, the latter choice usually
wins and there is a curtailment of children.

The newly-come foreigner, with his tradition
of children as an economic asset and, many
times looking forward to the day when his
children will support him, has no scruples as
to the standard of his children's living so long
as they have enough to eat and grow on. Later,
he may change his attitude and become sufficiently Americanized to want better things,

as so many have and do. But then he takes his place with the native-born in relation to our national birth-rate. You can doubtless point to cases where the very reverse is true. There are, of course, instances of exceedingly prolific families of native stock. But let us consider now in terms of statistical studies of our birth-rate, and in very general terms.

Suppose we had a smaller population in America now, due to an absence of immigration. Suppose we had only ninety millions, bred of our original colonial stock. Would our position in the world, or our relation to the World War have been very different? However, that is but speculation. There remains with us a very vital reality. Whatever might have happened in the past, there is the very real problem of what is going to happen in the future. We cannot undo the past, but we can anticipate what is to be.

America, tomorrow, will be made up of the grown babies of our native-born and foreign-born parents of today. The ratio of birth-rate stands about two to one in favor of the babies of the foreign-born. Facts and figures tell us that, as the foreign-born are assimilated and become Americanized, their birth-rate approaches that of the native-born. This means that, with immigration entirely cut off, the future would belong to descendants of a comparatively "American" stock, as our old blood still predominates in numbers, and the birth-rate tends to become the same for both groups.

But there seems little reason to close our gates entirely. We must anticipate a certain increment yearly from foreign lands. We must face the issue squarely and admit that America is going to belong, at least in large part, to the descendants of our foreign-born of to-day and those who come tomorrow. The question is, what kind of foreigners shall we select, whose children shall inherit their large share in the America that is to be? That question is practical, and its answer, in a measure, is practicable.

By raising our immigration standards, physical, mental, and moral, by enrolling all aliens admitted to this country and having them register yearly until they have become citizens, and by deporting all such as prove unworthy of American life and traditions, we can definitely raise the general average level of our population in point of physical fitness, intellectual stamina, and moral value.

"Selective Immigration or None" should be the motto of every American voter. To protect our country's future by a vote is a patriotic service just as much as to defend our country's present with a bayonet. Let us think of the America of tomorrow, as well as that of today.

CHAPTER XVII

FECUNDITY OF IMMIGRANT STOCK

England has been an emigrant nation for centuries. Englishmen have been pouring forth from the British Isles and spreading over the face of the world by the hundred thousand. They have settled in North America, South America, India, Egypt, and Africa in great colonies. Yet, since the time of Queen Elizabeth, when the great emigration began, the population of England has gone on steadily increasing at a normal rate until of recent years, when, like all highly civilized countries where the standard of living is high, it has suffered a decline in birth-rate.

History indicates that the drain of emigration from a country is usually made up in full by a rise in the birth-rate of that country. It also indicates that immigration into a new land causes a reduction in the birth-rate of the native stock of that land. This has been the case very notably in the United States, where the birth-rate of the foreign-born has always been higher than that of the native-born.

The governing principle in this phenomenon of humanity is economic. It is a matter of the standard of living. It used to be related largely to the marriage-rate. It is now related to both the marriage-rate and to voluntary birth-control.

When a group of families settle in an American community, willing to work at about half the prevailing wage-rate, and when their children go into factories in preference to school at the bidding of their parents, the whole economic life of that community is affected. The foreman says to the native-born worker that he can replace him on the job for less money. The native-born worker agrees to take a reduction in pay, or at least to refrain from asking higher wages. He curtails expenses. If he is single, he postpones marriage until a more propitious occasion. If he is married, he thinks twice before adding another child to his family, for he is too proud to regard children as mere food for the industrial mill; he has a higher standard than that for his children.

Meanwhile, the foreigner, brought up in the tradition of children as an economic asset, continues to bring children into that community at about twice the rate of the native population. The native-born element resents any downward pull on its standard of living, but, in a free country, where aliens may come and go as they please, the pull is inevitable and the only thing to do is to meet it. Postponement of marriage, or the limitation of families follows as a backfire to the menace of reduced standards for both parent and child.

These facts prove true wherever a careful investigation is made into the birth-rates of our native and foreign-born populations. Behind the figures, there always stands the economic problem of the standard of living, and this involves a difference in attitude and in ideals toward childhood. It is not that the native stock desires children less, nor is less fertile than the foreign stock. It is because the native-born has grown up into higher standards and ideals of what is due to children, and will not be content to give them the heritage of standards reduced to the level of incoming aliens of lands where standards of living are so much lower than ours.

Following are two studies, showing how very closely each approximates the other in the matter of proportional birth-rate. One is the study of births in New York, and the other of births in Massachusetts. Set these figures against the background of living standards that have been sketched in, and they become significant.

	Mass.	N. Y.
Births per 1000, native population	17.03	17.2
Births per 1000, foreign-born	52.16	43.7

Now there is not the slightest use lamenting such facts as these. Surely we cannot hold it against our foreign-born population that it desires children, and has them. What is already done we must face as a fact and let American institutions and ideals do their work upon our alien legion and attempt to Americanize it. But there is a very practical issue at hand when we anticipate the future.

What has been so in the past, and is now, is very likely to be tomorrow. If we cannot prevent the differential in birth-rate, the disproportion in numbers of children to our foreign-born and our native-born, if America is to belong largely to descendants of our foreign-element, then at least we ought to do what we can to see that this foreign population is sound and wholesome.

There is the individually selective principle which, when worked out in practical detail, will prove fairer to ourselves and to the people of other lands. On this principle, we shall welcome the better grades of all people not excluded by law. But they will have to prove themselves to be the kind of material of which we want America to be built. Our standards will be not only individual, but will go back into the families, into the heredity of our immigrants, for conclusions.

To some this may seem impractical as an immediate measure. It will be objected that we have no set standards, as yet, to make individual selection work. True enough, but rapid strides are being made in that direction. Already we can eliminate the obviously unfit to be citizens and the parents of citizens by birth. Tests and standards are evolving. Meanwhile we should take the best selective tests we have, and use them until we get a better set. We should shift the basis of our percentage law in accord with what seems best for our native population, even though the percentage basis be a rough and ready measure to tide over the period until we have a better way.

This is no time for quibbling over microscopic details of tests or percentages. It is a time for deliberate action, and for thorough investigation. We must discover just and honest methods for immigration tests and selection. We must see to it that immigration is so restricted as to make possible an approximate assimilation of aliens before they gather in huge, pasty lumps in our cities, and render the problem of the melting-pot impossible.

CHAPTER XVIII

THE BLOOD OF OUR FOUNDERS

Sickly, neurasthenic, psychopathic brains may have our pity and our treatment when they are found amongst us; but they must be kept from entering the United States on the plea that they are idealists, that they flee persecution, that they want to live in a land of free speech. Read the kind of manifesto they publish when they get here, in a fragment from one of these, as it was reprinted in the New York Times:

"We must mercilessly destroy all the remains of governmental authority and class domination . . . all legal papers pertaining to private ownership of property, all field fences and boundaries and burn all certificates of indebtedness—in a word, we must take care that everything is wiped out from the earth that is a reminder of the right of private ownership of property."

That sort of talk is not going to make a dent in any sane man's thinking. But the sort of mind that oozes it out lives in a body that will transmit that sort of mind to its children. It will not contaminate our American thinking so much as it will pollute the blood of the nation with more weak stock.

"There is perhaps no group in America so free from racial or religious prejudice as the workingman. It is a matter of indifference to him whether an immigrant comes from Great Britain, Italy, or Russia. The chief consideration is that, wherever he comes from, he shall be endowed with the capacity and imbued with the determination to improve his own status in life, and equally determined to preserve and promote the standard of life of the people among whom he expects to live."

These are the words of a laboring man, who became a labor leader in the United States. They express an idea and a sentiment that has taken root and is growing up in this Republic of ours and which is going to modify our whole national attitude toward the great problem of selective immigration.

"How long will the Republic endure? So long as the ideas of its founders remain dominant. How long will these ideas remain dominant? Just so long as the blood of its founders remains dominant in the blood of its people. Not the blood of the Puritans and Virginians alone, the original creators of free states, but the blood of free-born men, be they Greek, Roman, Frank, Saxon, Norman, Dane, Celt, Scot, or Goth. It is a free stock that creates a free nation. Our Republic shall endure as long as the human harvest is good, as long as the movement of history, the progress of science and industry, leaves for the future the best and not the worst of each generation."

These words, spoken by one of our great university presidents, make a fitting text from which to preach a little lay sermon.

It is conceded that the American people were all foreigners once. The American Indian is the only native that has a right to bewail the inheritance of America by foreigners. Columbus, Cortez, Miles Standish, John Smith, the Brewsters, Aldens, and Winthrops were foreigners. The big point is not one of race or nationality but of quality and breeding! Columbus was an Italian, Cortez a Spaniard, John Smith an Englishman, Peter Stuyvesant a Dutchman, and Von Steuben a German. We also have Irish, Welsh, French, Italian, Jewish, and Russian families in this country that have contributed sterling qualities to our composite American population. We want more of this kind and less of the kind that give us Jukes, Ishmaels, Kallikaks, and Nams that turn out human grist for Bolshevist parlors, anarchist newspapers, assassinations of the rich and of Presidents, and constitutional crepe hangers.

It has been suggested by members of the former Immigration Commission that if our Government were to keep abroad a confidential force to watch for criminal and immoral persons, and, we might add, persons of notably inferior heredity, who intended coming to America, there might be obtained interesting and valuable results. Our government does keep a force abroad to prevent smuggling of diamonds, silks, furs, and other dutiable articles. Why not take an equal, or even a greater amount of pains to spot and exclude dangerous and undesirable persons?

Furthermore, unless it can be proved that a person who commits a crime here has a criminal record in his own country, we cannot deport him. It would seem as though we should be able, by law, to deport an alien who turns criminal after arriving in the United States, at least within a reasonable period of years. He probably brought over a weakness and a tendency to commit crime, even though he may not have had a criminal record in his past.

Another point brought out by the Immigration Commission is that the "White Slave Traffic" is largely in the hands of aliens, and that the importation of persons from abroad for immoral purposes has become an organized industry. Since the revelations of the Commission, a great deal has been done to mitigate this evil, but we must not close our eyes to the fact that it still exists and needs rigorous attention.

The economic motive gave impulse to, and upholds this traffic. In bringing women to this country for immoral purposes, the role of wife or family relation is played so skilfully as to secure admission very often. It is difficult to keep such persons out, and equally difficult to spot and deport them after they are in.

Again, it would seem that the help of a corps of investigators at points of embarkation who could take time to look up the records of all immigrants to the United States would count valuably here. A great deal could be done abroad that cannot possibly be done once an immigrant lands at Ellis Island, or another of our own ports, where we have to accept the record they bring with them, their own statements, and their own personal condition.

To keep this nation clean, as in the days of its founders, to keep the best of all races and nationalities dominant that this nation may endure, we must watch our gates and select rigidly those who would come in. For, just as the blood of the Puritans, the Huguenots, the Dutch, the Germans, and the Scandinavian pioneers runs in the veins of our country, just so does the blood of the anarchist, the white-slaver, the irresponsible criminal pollute the stream of our national life. Just as we have fine types of Russian, Italian, Pole, Austrian, and South European added to our population by the later immigration, so, too, we have weak, unstable types from all these peoples.

Our immigration task is not to discriminate against one race or nationality or people, but against low types from every alien group which may seek America as its home. Just as surely as we find ways and means of exercising such selection rigidly and justly, just so certainly shall we realize the necessity for the rule of quality and solidarity of character as a test for those who would come among us to make their homes.

CHAPTER XIX

EFFECTS OF THE WORLD WAR

What type of immigrant may we expect as one of the results of the World War? Let us look at some of the forces at work among possible immigrants from Europe.

First, Europe forces a demand for reconstruction in industry and in building reparations. Industry in Europe makes its first drafts on the best, the sturdiest, the hardest workers, the best breeds. The same is true in building reparations. Food will long be at a premium. The type of European farmer who has stamina to work hard and long, who will stick to his plow or his hoe, who is ambitious, energetic, businesslike, finds it profitable to remain on his land.

The weak, the unambitious, the slacker type, finds it hard to get along. He is hungry and he is the first to be jobless. He is the first to listen to the call for cheap, unskilled labor in America, a call honeyed with talk of short hours, easy work, big pay. This is the type, the breed we may expect to see hovering around ports of departure. This is what we want to select against, keep out!

European governments want real men to stay at home and help build up a new civilization on the wreckage of the old. They want real women to remain at home, bear vigorous children, and provide food and shelter and comfort for the men of the nation and for its children. These governments are not going to encourage the emigration of good stock. They will discourage it. And while they may not actively assist in the departure of the jobless weak, the unstable of mind and nerve, the easily discontented and the constitutionally inferior, they need not be expected to stand in the way of such people taking passage for other lands! An official of one of the new republics in Europe frankly stated that his country's only concern with American immigration was the hope to get rid of the "old men and rubbish."

We are going to discover some day that cheap labor is the most costly in the long run. Nationally, we must pay altogether too high a price for getting some of our "dirty work" done cheaply. It is not even true that morons and high grade feeble-minders can dig ditches and lay crude stone walls and drive teams in a satisfactory manner. Should we not put America and the future of America first even were the cost of supervision of such labor not prohibitive?

Those who laid the foundations of the great ancient civilizations were vigorous, out-door men and women—called themselves *vires,* and men like those we call virile. There are thousands of such men in America today. And among the immigrants who come across seas there are still sound, vigorous men and women. There are men in our mills and on our farms a blow from whose fist is as powerful as a kick from a horse's hoof. There are women in our American homes who are built to bear fine children and who are strong and healthy enough to give these children the kind of home and training they need to become sterling citizens in body, mind, and spirit. It is to give these men and women a chance to found homes and raise healthy, wholesome, splendid children that we want to guard against their being swamped by the worthless spawn of the unfit, the weak, the unstable, the human stuff that ought never to be.

In France, of late years, there has been talk, even official talk, of bounties for marriage, of subsidizing children; of encouraging marriage and parenthood as a national duty. The low birth-rate of France has menaced the very continuance of France as a nation. So it was in ancient Rome after the Imperial Conquests. Race suicide was a bogey of the day. Senators advocated baby prizes and wedding gifts by the state. A prominent Roman declared that "marriage is a duty which, however painful, every citizen ought manfully to discharge." But it was all too late. Rome died "because the human harvest was bad."

The growth of America as a nation has not depended upon its birth-rate alone. Immigration has much more than made up for any decline in our rate of bearing children. There lies our great strength, and there too may lie our most fatal weakness. So long as we have room for immigrants, and capacity to assimilate them, just so long shall we grow in population despite a possible fall in birth-rate equal to that of France. But if we do not guard our gates carefully, if we do not see to it that only the fit, the strong, the men and women of good hereditary health come in, mere numbers will not save us from the fate of Rome, nor the tragedy of ancient Greece.

Our present literacy test, requiring an immigrant to read at least forty words in his own native tongue, must be regarded as an emergency measure. It has not been in effect long enough to enable us to form any complete deductions as to its benefits. This test may easily place a handicap upon immigrants from rural districts, upon men and women of the sturdy farmer types, but it may place a premium upon the city type which is more apt to have picked up a smattering of reading ability.

It is the city loafer, the shifter, the job loser, the mal-content who is most likely to be drifting about in Europe looking for high wages and little work. He will not find high wages in Europe, but he will find lots of work, too much for his kind. It is this type of man that bites at bootleg immigration bait, who is stowed away or otherwise slipped through into America to join the Communists, "I Won't Works," and "I Trouble-you Trouble-yous." Let us thank the literacy test, let us thank our 2 per cent quota law, let us thank our faithful immigration officials for what each has done toward saving us from the results of the last great wave of immigration to threaten our shores. Let us be glad that men and women in other lands have come to people America. Let us be ever ready to welcome more. But let us intelligently raise our standards of admission to the United States to fit the standards we maintain here, not only of living, but also of sound heredity.

While continuing to enforce laws that will limit the actual total numbers to come to us from other lands, let us at the same time strengthen our selective tests of the individual as he or she comes and say "No!" to those who do not measure up. Every race, every representative of every foreign nation now in America will benefit by this, for America will become a better and a happier place for each one of us to live in just in proportion as we raise and keep high the standard of life in terms of personal fitness and of personal character.

CHAPTER XX

A LOOK INTO THE FUTURE

Suppose that when the next war-alarm sounds, some one should get up and make a speech in behalf of preserving our best American families. Suppose he should advocate sending to the front our weak-minded, insane, paupers, criminals, anarchists, and theoretical reformers instead of the best fighting blood we possess in the nation. Suppose he should argue that by doing this we would leave the best men at home to become the fathers of the next generation, and get rid of our socially unfit and those whom we do not want to see multiply in the land. You would probably dismiss him as a genial idiot not even worth locking up as a danger to enlistment or to the draft.

Still, there may be found in some of the wildest vaporizations of our soap-box orators an occasional morsel of food for thought worth chewing over, and this question of the effects of war on parenthood and on coming generations seems to call for some little Fletcherizing. Let us consider some of its suggestions.

In the countries from which our foreign-born population has come there were born, during and immediately after the World War, millions of new babies. These babies are now growing up into men and women. Many thousands of them are being fed with American food, clothed with American cotton and wool, and helped back into health with American medicine and medical care. America is getting into their small heads. They are beginning now to think about the United States and they will be thinking about that far off country when they are old enough to look for a job.

And just as they are now looking into the future, and perhaps dreaming of some day coming to America, let us look into the future and try to picture what sort of men and women this crop of war-babies is likely to be. One of the best ways of looking into the future is to first glance at the past. History is not only a record of what has happened, but is often a prophetic reflector of what may be again. That history repeats itself is no idle fiction. In a great many important cases it is a grim and solid fact.

Napoleon Bonaparte called on the best blood of France to rally 'round his banners of conquest. Campaign after campaign drew heavier and heavier draughts on the youth and vigor of France. Six hundred thousand men followed him into Russia, and about twenty thousand came back with him in retreat. He called for more soldiers for more campaigns, and when the age of recruits was reduced and reduced again, he merely said, "A boy can stop a bullet as well as a man." One of the many results of the Napoleonic Wars was a very distinct and noticeable decrease in the stature of the French nation as a whole. Height does not mean everything, but it is one of the indices of vigour and stamina when a whole race or nation is concerned.

Skip a few years, and we come to the Franco-Prussian war of 1870-1871. Military statistics, both German and French, show that the German and French babies born during that war, when they grew up to the age of military service were found to be distinctly inferior to the type registering for service that came from babies born before that conflict.

Again, the Japanese draft soldiers of 1915 were found by Japanese military authorities to be of notably delicate constitution, inferior to the usual run of soldiers admitted to the Japanese army. Looking back over their birth records, it was found that these draft soldiers were born during and immediately after the almost forgotten war between China and Japan, when the young and vigorous men were at the front, and the old men, and the weak, and the too young stayed at home and became parents of the soldiers to be.

Twenty, thirty years from now the babies born during the terrible strain of the World War, children for the most part of those who were not fit to be at the front, will be among the immigrants coming to America. We want those who come to us to become citizens, to contribute homes, families, children, to our commonwealth. We must think in these terms, now, when framing our laws for admission or rejection of those who are to become the Americans of tomorrow.

We cannot wait twenty or thirty years to

see what results the war will have had on the breed of European manhood and womanhood. We cannot wait until then to decide what tests, what standards we shall hold up to those who would come to America. Then it will be too late. Now is the time to act, both for the present, for ourselves and our children, and for the future, for our grandchildren.

Our emergency immigration law has been designed to save us from the immediate results of the war in a possible overflow from Europe of countless men and women. What we need now is an intelligent, thoroughly built law, and adequate machinery for its enforcement, looking not only to the present and the near future, but to the welfare of the America which is to be.

The demoralization of European industry, the destruction of property and the breaking up of homes, multiplied taxation, fear of further war, hopelessness, and despair all coupled with the vision of America as a Land of Promise are motives that have driven great multitudes to the desire to emigrate from their homeland. We were threatened with a great tidal wave of immigration after the World War, despite restrictive measures on the part of some European governments, wishing to keep their men at home for reconstruction.

We met this problem by emergency immigration laws, the quota acts. But we must look farther than the immediate present. We must formulate an immigration policy that will work now, and work down the years into the future. It must be a selective policy, aiming to admit to this Republic only the best, only the sound of all those peoples who will press to come across seas. And this will be more especially true twenty years from now than it is even today.

CHAPTER XXI

THREE JEWISH MIGRATIONS

If, in your own home town, you felt in constant danger of being hauled into a dark cellar, put through the third degree by men in long black robes and masks, and then sentenced to slow torture or painful death, would you not be tempted to emigrate to safer regions? If you had to choose between the chance of being laid out on a rack which would crack your joints apart, and the chance of getting shipwrecked at sea, would you not choose the shipwreck? If you had the choice of having your feet put into iron boots while hot lead was poured in, or of meeting an Indian with a tomahawk in the woods, would you not prefer the Indian? If you had before you the certainty of at least experiencing the sensation of thumbscrews or hot coals, and the chance of having to fight a big brown bear, would you not risk the bear?

Well, so did large numbers of Spanish Jews, back in the days when little brick houses and

Dutch wind-mills stood on the present site of the Bowling Green building and the New York customs house. If these men had an economic motive in coming to America, it was probably secondary to the fear of torture and sudden death at the hands of the Inquisition. But not only did these Spanish Jews come because they chose; multitudes were expelled from Spain at about the time of the discovery of America and, wandering to other lands, they later heard of the New World, and began crossing the sea. It was from this branch of the Jewish race and religion, a branch characterized by many of the finest qualities, that America was partly settled before our War of the Revolution.

The Inquisition followed them into those parts of America that were controlled by Spain, so that gradually more and more of these persecuted people came to New Amsterdam, Philadelphia, and Boston. Here they gradually became Americans, by language, custom, and largely by marriage. Their descendants, even while keeping some of the old Spanish names, have gradually melted into our population of merchants, bankers, importers, exporters, artists, and scholars.

Later came the German Jews, whose principal period of immigration was from 1815 to 1880, with a time of special pressure during the late '40's when there was religious and revolutionary trouble at home. They were men and women of somewhat different type from the Spanish Jew, and brought over a new set of traditions in business and social life. They brought with them the aptitude for adjustment to a great variety of possible conditions at which one could make a living and get a start in life. They were a much poorer group, financially, than the Spanish Jews, and had to make their beginnings lower down on the scale of material welfare. That America spelled opportunity for them is witnessed by the climb from small, itinerant clothing merchants to great owners of department stores and banks, as exemplified in the careers of Benjamin Altman, the Seligmans, and the brothers Straus.

The German Jews of this early immigration did not settle in city colonies. They were fairly distributed throughout our cities, and throughout the country, mainly as traveling merchants, small store-men, and private bankers. They assimilated slowly, but noticeably, with the native stock, learned English readily, and became an organic part of the life of the Republic in all but religion, which it was their right to keep distinctive and separate, as it is the right of each of us.

The success of these German Jews in America had no little to do with the opening up of that great reservoir of some nine million Jews who live in the territory of the old Kingdom of Poland. This region of the world is the real homeland of the Jew. In comparison to the number of Jews living in old Poland there is only a scattered handful in the rest of the world, except in the United States, where there are now about three million. Half of this number live in Greater New York.

"If the American government should take ten million of its citizens, drive them into the cities of New England, prohibit them from living anywhere else, oblige them to follow certain occupations, forbid them to own land, and heap upon them numerous other restrictions from which the mass of the population was free," says Mr. Burton Hendrick, "we should reproduce a condition which resembles the existence of the Jews in Russia during the early eighties and nineties when the great new immigration into America began."

When these people heard of America, a land where they could come and go as they wished, own their homes, take up whatever occupation they preferred, the great migration began. It was stimulated, perhaps initiated, by persecutions and pogroms following the assassination of Czar Alexander II, but it continued because the homeland Jews had discovered another "Promised Land."

Mr. Hendrick has stated that the Jews of mark and prominence in America are almost exclusively from the stock we know as German Jews, with a small sprinkling from the old Spanish-Jewish blood. Of the former, the names Lewisohn, Kahn, Wolf, Guggenheim, Warburg, Schiff, Straus, Stern, Gimbel, Altman, Speyer, Goldman, Sachs, Hallgarten, Untermeyer, and Meyer, from the business, banking, and legal fields, and Oscar Straus, Louis Brandeis, Abraham Elkus, and Eugene Meyer, from the field of public positions are examples. Of the latter stock Bernard Baruch and Benjamin Cardozo are mentioned.

Perhaps it is too early to judge the contribution of the later immigrant stock, coming mostly from southeastern Europe. It takes

time for a man, or for a people, to make good
in a new land. The fact is that all three strains
of Jews are actually in America. The fact
remains that it is obviously our duty to protect these, as well as our people as a whole,
from the incoming of any inferior types of
men and women, Jew or Gentile. That is the
drive of selective immigration, a policy which
America must adopt in the interests of her
future welfare.

It is stated that the Jews from the region
that was formerly Poland are of still a different type from either the Spanish Jew or
the German Jew of the earlier migration.
There has been considerable speculation as to
the relative merits of these types. Anthro-
pologists and statisticians agree or disagree;
but one practical issue remains clear. From
every race and people there come to America
specimens of good blood, and specimens of
bad blood. Whatever general type may come,
there is a choice between individuals and families within that type; and this choice should
be ours to make. Preferably the choice should
be made in the land from which these people
come, instead of after their voyage to our
shores. It is fairer to them, and to us.

We want to welcome the kind of immigrant who, even though he begin, like Benjamin Altman, with a pack on his back, climbs up to a position of respect and civic value in his community. An intelligent basis for selective immigration will help us get that kind of person. It will take more time, it will mean more expense, but it will be worth a thousand times the time and expense to the future of this Republic. Let us have selective immigration, or none.

CHAPTER XXII

DISTINGUISHED IMMIGRANTS

It has been estimated that, based on the natural increase of our native American stock, the United States would have a population of about one hundred million today if no immigrants had ever come to this country since the year 1800. The fact that immigrants did come, it has been shown, brought about a reduction in the native birth-rate, which is now about one half the birth-rate of our foreign-born.

What might have happened, no one will ever know. What did happen we have some record concerning. Immigrants did come, and certain of these immigrants influenced our history profoundly. Without guessing as to what our native stock alone might have produced in the way of nation builders had it been left to itself, let us briefly review some of the outstanding figures brought over to America on the immigration tides.

Not to go back into colonial days, or the

early pioneering of the founders of our Nation, let us consider here a few true emigrants from their homelands, and immigrants to our United States. Where would our science of botany, zoology, and geology, stand today had not Louis Agassiz found such a hearty welcome when he came to America from Switzerland in 1846 that he decided to remain here, found a home, and devote his genius to work in American fields?

Henry Astor settled in New York shortly after our Revolutionary days, and wrote home about the wonderful opportunities of the New World. John Jacob, his brother, read these letters, caught his brother's enthusiasm, packed up, came over, and started modestly in the fur business. His wife and he lived over their little fur-shop, where he sold musical instruments as a side line, until they had saved enough money to consider it safe to move into a house of their own. The Waldorf Astoria is named half for the little German town from which the Astors came, and half for a family whose name is indelibly written in the economic history of the Republic. Germany also sent us August Belmont, lamed for life in a duel, but a thorough sportsman in business and re-creation and a philanthropist at heart.

Alexander Graham Bell was too restless to remain even in the airy freedom of mountainous Scotland, and came over to teach in Boston University back in 1872. We need only to refer to the history of the telephone in America for a liberal education in what this honored Scotsman contributed to the civilization of the world.

James Gordon Bennett found proof-reading in Boston more attractive than apprenticeship in his little Scottish town of New Mill, near Keith, and so he came across the ocean, resolved to become a publisher. He wrote the first copies of "The Herald" himself, and built up this newspaper into a national institution.

Another Scot, this time from Dunfermline, came over with his father, a poor weaver, in 1845. His first job was tending a small stationary engine. Then he stepped from telegraph messenger to telegraph clerk, met Woodruff, inventor of the sleeping-car, made some money through that invention, invested wisely, took to iron and steel and gave us the material out of which Mr. Morgan welded together the

United States Steel Corporation, the largest employer of immigrant labor in America. To-day, Andrew Carnegie, self-made immigrant American, is held up before audiences of possible radicals by proselyting agitators as the arch type of a terrible and grinding capitalism that would crush all individuality, all initiative, all hope for a better world of men!

Likewise the agitator points to Wall Street, crying out against its tyranny over the working class and the poor immigrant, forgetting, however, to point out the firm of Drexel and Co., founded by Francis M. Drexel, who emigrated, a persecuted political refugee from the Austrian Tyrol, and landed on our shores in 1817 to make himself a name and fortune by his own effort and native worth.

M. Du Pont de Nemours, Sr., born in Paris, member of the States-General of the French Revolutionary time, mobbed, nearly killed, imprisoned, liberated, raised high in political life again, once more imprisoned, his house pillaged and burned, finally emigrated to America. Here he wrote an educational platform for President Jefferson, contributed original thought to American politics and statesmanship, and founded one of the great families of the United States.

Some people contend that our immigration standards should be kept low because we cannot spot a potential Bell or Carnegie or Steinmetz at our gates, and had better take a chance on getting one man of rare ability even while chancing the admission of a host of possible undesirables. But let us hope to see our immigration tests and examinations based on character, energy, native ability, qualities not to be measured by an ordinary "mental test" which tries out only acquired ability of mind. No sound man or woman of whatever potential quality in ability or genius will then be debarred, and the elimination of the unsound and the unwholesome in body, mind, or character, will mean just that much more chance for the good to work its way up into the light of real prosperity and success, measured not in mere terms of money, but of service to the nation.

A few distinguished American immigrants who have illumined our nation's history and helped set high standards of progress, achievement, and ideals have been mentioned. Another "foreigner", whose brain, like that of

Steinmetz (also an immigrant) and Edison (a native son) kept running at high speed throughout his life in the practical service of his fellow men is John Ericsson.

He was a good surveyor at fourteen years of age, in Sweden, but caught a vision of America as the land of promise for mechanical genius. He emigrated and began to turn out new inventions of real usefulness with the speed and system of a multigraph or an adding machine. What concerned the history of our Republic most was the revolving turret for battleships and the screw propeller for steamships. John Ericsson revolutionized ocean-travel and naval warfare. The screw propeller was to steam navigation what the age of bronze axes was to the age of stone hatchets. The revolving turret was to the clumsy ship's broadside as gunpowder and shot to bow and arrow, and spear and shield.

Ericsson not only invented the revolving turret. One hundred days after his plans for the little "Monitor" were approved by Congress he had built and launched that memorable gunboat and got it into Hampton Roads just in time to keep the steel-rail clad "Merrimac" from completing the destruction of the best part of our United States Navy. The whole outcome of the Civil War was doubtless changed by this momentous battle between the first iron ships. The small "cheese-box on a raft," which could move its guns without having to move its hull, made short work of the big, solid iron-clad, with gun-range limited by its own position. Invention had been met with better invention, and the step from wooden ship to iron-armored had led to the turret type of battle ship which has been adopted and modified by all the navies of the world.

Ericsson also gave us the first torpedo, or under-water gun as it was called at the time, besides a whole cataract of minor naval devices such as sounding instruments, gun-locks, gun carriages, shock-absorbers, fluid gauges, etc. in addition to his steam-engines, sun-motors, and heating devices. Sweden was proud of her son, as America has been proud in his adoption.

John W. Mackay came over from Ireland back in 1840. He got a job in a shipyard, worked hard and hoped to be a shipyard boss some day. But the gold-rush to California began and John went along. He made a small fortune and lost it. But he got to work again. Working as a miner in his own mine, paying his men their wages even when a fire wiped out all income from the mine itself, he finally struck the great bonanza vein from which his partners and he took out some $150,000,000 in gold and silver.

That was luck plus hard work and persistence and decent treatment of workmen. But Mr. Mackay did more than make a fortune. He used it in the development of America. It is not necessary to go into details, only to mention his laying, with James Gordon Bennett, another of our alien-born citizens, of two Atlantic cables, one to England and one to France. His energy, his native ability, his money, all went into the building of America which is your heritage and mine. Not even a goldmine is a gift of the gods. To dig gold takes work, and sweat, and risk, and dogged persistence. Making the right use of gold takes higher qualities still. It has been these higher qualities that have made America great.

If we were to glance over an encyclopedia of American biography published before 1890, we should be impressed with the sprinkling of foreign-born men and women who have come across the sea to make their home with us, and give us the best they had. A few more whose history has become so much a part of us that it needs no retelling are: John Drew, from Ireland; Joseph Jefferson, Sr., from Plymouth, England; Frank Leslie, from Ipswich, England; Stephen Girard, from Bordeaux, France; August Gemunder, violin-maker from Wurttemberg, Germany; and Luigi Gregori, decorator of cathedrals, who brought his fine art from Bologna, Italy, to enrich our churches.

John Roebling left Muhlhausen, Prussia; and we have the great Niagara suspension bridge, a score of other splendid bridges across our rivers and, completed by his gifted son, the wonderful Brooklyn Bridge, for a long time one of the architectural and engineering wonders of the world. William Rittenhause, of Holland, gave us our first paper mill and set Dutch standards, perhaps the highest in the world, for the making of our best papers.

From Budapest, Hungary, a young man, Joseph Pulitzer, came to New York, learned English quickly, picked an eminent foreign-born citizen, Carl Schurz, as his master and took to journalism. He built up the "New York World." His success as a newspaper man was greatly helped along by the fact that another immigrant American, Robert Hoe, had landed in the United States in 1803 and devoted himself to the perfection of the cylinder press. The Hoe press is now almost as important an element in our national economy and progress as the telegraph or the telephone.

And so we might go on indefinitely, picking samples of immigrants who have done their bit in the building of our nation. To repeat what has been so often said before, if we would make this country a land of truly free-born and free-bred people, a true democracy in spirit as well as in name, we must take greater care what sort of immigrants come in. Selective immigration laws, if truly selective, will not keep out the able, the ambitious, the sound of blood. It will encourage the coming of such, and discourage, and finally abolish immigration of the kind of person who becomes a drag, instead of a lift, to our Republic.

CHAPTER XXIII

SUBSTANTIAL IMMIGRANTS

Moses was a wise old leader of an immigrant people. He not only set up a wonderful sanitary code for people on the march, and in camp, and gave them a set of moral and civic laws that have become the background for millions of human beings, but he also saw to it that the genealogy of his people was written down and preserved. He was jealous of the racial purity of his people. He was prideful in the family and tribal tradition. His scribes recorded not alone the brilliant and distinguished, but all the solid backbone of the nation, by family and by name.

We have in the United States no such unity of family stock. Our Republic is the most stupendous experiment in racial intermixture that the world has ever seen. One hardly dares guess what the resultant product of this huge melting pot will be. Genealogies of the wealthy and prominent alone are carefully recorded, save in rare instances of devotion to a family tree among those who cannot well afford the services of a genealogist. Only of late years has such an institution as the Eugenic Record Office begun the work of collecting and filing family histories of representative America; and its work lies almost entirely in the future. Its history lies before it.

But our encyclopedias of American biography, our "Who's Who," and scattered records of achievement, all attest the fact that immigration has brought to America individuals and families of staunch civic worth. Some of the more distinguished of our immigrant Americans have been mentioned. Let us consider just a few random samples of those whom we might call our substantial immigrants, not merely those who have made money, but those who have genuinely contributed a man's share to the building of the commonwealth.

Lewis Feuchtwanger, for instance, came to us from Bavaria and persuaded our government that nickel could be used to advantage in coining small change. George Bruce followed his brother from Scotland and gave us the best specimen of type-casting machine ever made, and one which is now in general use. The beauty and clearness of his cut types, and various inventions and improvements have worked steadily for the raising and keeping high our American standards of the printer's art.

Dr. Brown Sequard, migrating to America from the Island of Mauritius, contributed a vast amount of knowledge and skill to the progress of American medicine, especially in the study of the blood-stream and the nervous system. Junius Brutus Booth preferred America to London, bought a farm near Baltimore, and set standards for our stage that we have found it difficult to live up to. He gave us Edwin Booth who made Hamlet famous and showed us how we might keep up stage standards.

Mathew Carey sailed from Ireland to bring his gospel of religion for young folks to the United States. He founded our first Sunday-School Society and became a dynamic center of quiet, educational moral reform. This is what we need in greater abundance instead of the multitude of societies and ilks and isms that rest their faith on compulsions, prohibitions, censorships, and the making of petty laws for the regulation of human conduct.

Two stories of later arrivals, who typify the spirit we want to see representative in every immigrant who lands on our shores are as follows: A young German in Saxony decided that it would be worth while to come to America. He came as far as Eau Claire, Wisconsin, bought 120 acres of land, and went back to fetch his wife and children. Finding that only 50 of the 120 acres were fit for crops, he saw he had been cheated, as the whole farm had been sold him as first class farm land. But instead of cursing America and Americans, he went to work.

At first his crops were the poorest in the neighborhood. After years of intensive work they were the best. He sold eggs at the rate of three dozen for a quarter, and butter at fifteen cents a pound. But he got ahead. He was glad to be in America, glad to stay. He took out citizenship papers. He was made road commissioner and elected to the school board. When he was elected town clerk he found he would have to study English and get a better grip on the language. At fifty-five he dug into grammar, and rhetoric, and composition, and mastered English for all practical purposes.

He was re-elected to office as town clerk for five years running, usually by a unanimous vote.

A Swede came to America in 1871. He left a job as a hired farmhand where he worked from four in the morning until eight at night and had to walk eight miles to his porridge supper and a few hours of rest. He got to Chicago where he dug graves for a living, and then worked on the railroad until he married a Swedish girl and bought a twenty-acre farm with the money he had saved. It is not necessary to give his whole life history. It is summed up in the one word work. Thrift, honesty, and persistent ambition to better his condition and that of his family entered into the composition, but his work is what counted in getting started. He sold his little farm, bought a larger one and then a larger one still. He reported to the Swedish Immigration Commission that he owned 300 acres of land, a sawmill, two stores, and eight city houses. Besides this, he brought up eight children, every one of whom had an example of what sound nerves, firm will, reasonable ambition, and sterling character will bring to an alien immigrant in America who will accept America for what it is, and work.

These cases are typical of the substantial immigrant of recent years in favor of whom we would have our selective immigration machinery strengthened. It is for this kind of stranger that the proposed enrollment of aliens, with its accompanying advantages in the way of education for citizenship, would prove helpful. Men of this type have nothing to fear from raised standards of admission to America, or from any suspicion of espionage in a plan designed only to help advance their progress toward a true Americanization.

The way in which good blood runs through the veins of a nation is illustrated in the contributions made to our country by various national stocks who have added great names to the American roll of honor. Take, for example, a few names of men proud of their French-Huguenot ancestry. Beginning with Paul Revere and Alexander Hamilton, we come down through John Bowdoin, Richard Dana, John Jay, Admiral Dupont, General Fremont, Admiral Dewey, and Winfield Scott Schley. Presidents Tyler, Garfield, and Roosevelt, and our poets Whittier and Longfellow likewise derive from this stock. Andrew Jackson was proud of his Scotch-Irish ancestry, and so were James Polk, James Buchanan, Andrew Johnson, Chester A. Arthur, William McKinley, Benjamin Harrison, and Grover Cleveland.

Previously have been set down the names of famous German-derived Americans and the contributions made to our history by men of Italian, Austrian, Dutch, British, and other racial stocks. Let us now select the Welsh as an illustration of a people's role in the building of a new nation.

Roger Williams came from Wales to America about 140 years before our Declaration of Independence and established a little democracy on the site of our present city of Providence, Rhode Island. A little later, William Penn, also of Welsh origin, founded the City of Brotherly Love.

Thomas Jefferson echoed the spirit of his Welsh ancestry when he declared that "rebellion to tyrants is obedience to God." Among other men of Welsh blood who joined him in signing the Declaration of Independence were John Hancock, Samuel and John Adams, Francis Lewis, Stephen Hopkins, William Williams, Lewis Morris, John Penn, and William Morris who gave his whole great fortune and died poor in the cause of liberty for America.

Welsh blood also played its appointed part in our history through Presidents Monroe, Harrison, Lincoln, and Garfield. Jefferson Davis, truly Welsh in devotion to his convictions, and believing he was right, sacrificed his career as Secretary of War, and became President of the Confederacy.

In American education, as well as in politics, Welsh stock has contributed its quota. John Harvard, Elihu Yale, and Colonel Williams each founded a college now become an American tradition. Brown University was established by Morgan Edwards and Samuel Jones, and our Philips Exeter and Philips Andover Academies grew out of an idea in the head of yet another Welshman, John Phillips.

These men, who were immigrants or the descendants of immigrants of Welsh blood, have contributed to the upbuilding of our Republic. In our coal mines, steel mills, and great factories, on our farms, and in thousands of typical American working-men's homes, the spirit of Wales, the spirit of freedom and of industry has done and is doing its appointed work. The use of the Welsh in America is merely a concrete illustration of what the immigrant blood of one people has contributed to the founding and perpetuation of a new nation. The word immigrant is used in the sense of an immigrant stock transplanted from its native land to a new country where it has settled and become a part of the whole.

Previously have been pointed out some of the weakening, undermining, and polluting results of admitting weak blood and unsound stock to our nation. The Welsh in America have taken a strong and even an official stand against any undesirable Welshmen coming to America. Their press gives them their national news and while their old people and their late arrivals keep up their language and many of their old customs, music, and song, they Americanize rapidly. They feel that they fit. They have found their place and want to make it the best sort of place they know how. With all loyalty and love for their native land, they come to put America first when they become Americans.

That is the sum and substance of true Americanization. Other people also find it the best and happiest way to do. Let us trust that all people who come here will find it so. They will if they are the right kind; if they respond; if they fit. The way to get responsive people here from other lands, the way to bring folks who will fit, find their place in our great, dynamic scheme of things and be happy in contributing their share to a national purpose, is to select them on a basis before they come. Native character, native background in solidity and wholesomeness, and native ability to respond to the new environment constructively, should be our tests of fitness to come in.

We want the beaver type of man. We want to keep out the rat-type. In order to do this, we must have a thoroughly workable basis for the operation of selective immigration.

CHAPTER XXIV

CONCLUSION

Out of the facts and figures set forth in this book we are able to reach certain conclusions as to the measures to be taken to solve the immigration problem and the problem of the alien within the United States. The matter of numerical restriction on legislation is of course one that lies entirely with the Congress of the United States. But it is clear that any numerical restriction imposed, whether in the nature of quota limitation or otherwise, should apply to all foreign countries alike. Our experience in exempting British North America, Mexico, Central and South America from all quota limitation has proved disastrous. It has had the effect of closing the front door to immigration and leaving the back door wide open. It has provided machinery and methods for the smuggler, the bootlegger of immigrants who links this trade with the illicit traffic in rum and narcotic drugs. It has practically put a premium on illegal entry into the United States.

Under it nearly sixty-five thousand Mexicans entered this country in one year, bringing into American communities lower standards of living.

It is true that Congress has enacted and is considering many measures which are important steps forward in the solution of the problem of the alien. They will help, but our real need is a comprehensive, effective, workable code of laws which will provide for immigration control, and will establish proper relations between the aliens in the United States, the government, and our citizens.

There is a persistent demand for relaxation of immigration limitation for economic reasons. The plea is continually made that we need labor, particularly common labor, in order that our industries may be kept fully manned. But it is a fact that many of our industries are already overmanned, and that in many others the substitution of up-to-date machinery and methods would eliminate much of the need for man power. The bituminous coal mining industry, for example, is both overdeveloped and overmanned. Many mines work on part time, many will sooner or later be forced to close down. It is estimated that there are 250,000 more bituminous coal miners in the mines than are needed to supply the country with coal. As a result the whole industry works on a short week, sometimes operating only two or three days out of seven. If those extra 250,000 could be placed in other industries needing man power the remaining miners would be able to earn six days' pay a week, and the mines could operate continuously. The industries to which these men would transfer their labor would likewise benefit. If all of our steel plants were on the same basis as our most efficient plants, we could produce all the iron and steel we need with one-third the present number of men.

The economic argument cannot be met by simply throwing down the bars for the indiscriminate admission of immigrants. By that system we would not get the men we need at the time we need them. In the light of these conditions, and in the light of the importance of immigration as a matter of breeding future Americans, there should be provision made for a selective immigration system, with an initial examination of all applicants before they start across the sea. This would be accomplished by requiring every prospective immigrant to obtain from the American consular office near-est his home an immigration certificate, based upon a verified questionnaire to be filed by the applicant and checked by competent immigra-tion and Public Health Service officials attached to the consular offices. The immigration certifi-cate would be issued only when the applicant had made clear his admissibility under the immigra-tion laws of the United States. The issuance of certificates to these classes of immigrants should be provided for giving preference to the hus-bands, wives, minor children and fathers and mothers of alien residents in this country who have declared their intention to become citizens of the United States. After these have been cared for, certificates should be issued to all other immigrants who could qualify, within any quota limitation imposed.

There should be a provision for the admis-sion to the United States regardless of quota limitation, if the quota is exhausted, of the husband, wife, minor child, or dependent father or mother of a citizen of the United States. This could be taken care of through Special Immigration Certificates to be issued at the direction of the Secretary of Labor upon the verified showing of the citizen of the United States seeking to have his relative or relatives admitted that he is able to provide for them properly.

Through this same Special Immigration Certificate could be met our economic needs for man-power. Provision should be made for the issue of such certificates, as preferences within quota limitations, for the admission of farmers and skilled or unskilled labor, where labor of like kind cannot be found in the United States, provided no strike or lockout exists or impends in the industry seeking to import such labor. This plan should be safeguarded by provision for full and ample hearing and investigation by the Secretary of Labor into the conditions under which it is sought to bring labor into the country. To balance this provision for selecting man power, authority should be vested in the President of the United States, by proclamation, to suspend immigration for the time, in the manner, and to the extent necessary whenever the Secretary of Labor and the Secretary of Commerce shall jointly certify that in their opinion unemployment in this country makes suspension necessary. We have seen the need for such suspension. Following the close of the war, millions of American workers were without employment. Despite our hastily imposed quota limitation, thousands of alien workers were admitted to the United States only to be added to the army of idleness and to become a burden on American industry.

To supplement this system of selective immigration, there should be provided a plan to aid the alien after he has reached our shores. Such a plan might be the organization of a great "Uncle Sam's Fraternity" with every alien in this country enrolled. Through this fraternity would be provided education in the language, customs, ideals, and standard of living of America for every alien. This could be accomplished by enlisting the aid of our churches, schools, patriotic, civic, and fraternal organizations in this great work of making better citizens, and better parents for citizens of the future. At the head of this great fraternity would be placed the President of the United States. This fraternity would be financed through an annual fee to be paid by the alien, which would be remitted in the case of an individual unable to meet the payment. Thus the rich alien, and there are many of them in this country, who would not need the educational facilities provided, would help to provide them for the less fortunate alien.

There is nothing radical or revolutionary in this proposal. It is based upon a principle always recognized in our American scheme of things. Every American citizen must register to qualify himself to vote. Practically every state in the Union provides for compulsory education of our children, both native-born and alien. We insist that the alien child must learn to know America and American ways, but we leave that child's parents to struggle for what knowledge of their new land they can pick up among their own neighbors, often aliens themselves, unfamiliar with the land of their adoption. By an annual census, and the issuance of an alien enrollment card, the present method of naturalization, under which the alien is at a tremendous disadvantage, and which often proves expensive and difficult, would be simplified. The enrollment card in "Uncle Sam's Fraternity" would be a record of the alien's life in America, and would be ample evidence for naturalization after the alien had completed the required term of residence.

This system, too, would enable us to weed out the alien who has entered the country in violation of the law, or who is here to preach the downfall of our institutions, the overthrow of all law and order. It would provide help for the alien who seeks to become a real American, and would check the activity of the alien who is here for no good purpose. An alien unable to produce an enrollment card would be given an opportunity to appear before a truly American group in his own community, and if he demonstrated that he preferred another government to ours, we could help him find such a government.

These proposals are put forward in the interests of the immigrant who comes to us from abroad, the alien who is within our gates, and all American citizens, today and in the future.

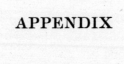

APPENDIX

APPENDIX A

SUMMARY OF IMMIGRANT LEGISLATION

Immigration to America was practically unrestricted and unregulated until the year 1819. Previous to that date there had been protests of individual governors of states against the dumping of criminals upon their people, but nothing like an immigration policy or law on the part of the Federal Government was approached.

From 1819 on there have been various proposed bills and acts leading in recent years to a more or less definite immigration policy. Chronologically these are as follows:—

1819—Regulation of carriage of steerage passengers at sea.

Provision for keeping statistics and records regarding immigration.

1836—State Department directed to collect information on immigration of foreign paupers and criminals.

1838—A congressional committee requested to report on expediency of revising the naturalization laws and the restriction of vagabonds and paupers. No legislation.

1847—Better steerage conditions required by law.

1855—Further regulation of steerage conditions.

1864—Commissioner of Immigration appointed.

Foreign labor contracts validated to encourage immigration after Civil War.

1866—Additional Commissioners of Immigration stationed on Atlantic Coast.

Congressional protest against dumping of criminals and undesirables upon the United States.

1868—Law of 1864 favoring immigration of contract labor repealed.

1875—Prostitutes excluded by law.

1876—Culmination of a movement for national control whereby federal control of immigrant legislation was made supreme.

1882—First general immigration law. Head tax fifty cents.

Convicts (except political), lunatics, idiots, and those to become public charges excluded.

Provision for better steerage conditions.

1885—Importation of contract labor forbidden.

No provision made for detection or deportation of contract laborers.

1887—Secretary of the Treasury given authority to deport within the year any immigrant landed contrary to this law.

1889—Standing Congressional Committee on Immigration established to investigate immigration and working of immigration laws.

1891—Persons loathsomely or dangerously diseased, and polygamists excluded.

Solicitation of immigrant labor prohibited.

Names, nationality, and personal details regarding immigrants to be filed.

Examination on Mexican and Canadian borders provided for.

Aliens landed in violation of immigration laws deportable within one year.

1893—Head tax raised to $1.00.

1897—President Cleveland vetoed educational test.

1898—Industrial Commission appointed to investigate immigration and suggest legislation.

1903—Head tax raised to $2.00.

Exclusion of insane, or persons insane within five years, or who have had two attacks of insanity, epileptics, professional beggars, and anarchists.

Illegal to assist entrance of anarchists.

Department of Commerce and Labor organized.

Commissioner General of Immigration appointed to administer immigration laws under that Department.

1906—Uniform rule for naturalization of aliens.

Bureau of immigration called Bureau of Immigration and Naturalization.

1907—Head tax raised to $4.00.

Exclusion of imbeciles, feeble-minded, unaccompanied children under seventeen, physically or mentally defective, prostitutes or prospective prostitutes.

Lists of outgoing passengers required of steamships.

Immigration Commission created.

President empowered to call International Conference on Immigration and to revoke passports of aliens entering to detriment of labor conditions in United States.

1910—Punishment and deportation provided for aliens profiting from prostitution.

1913—President Taft vetoed literacy test.

1915—President Wilson vetoed literacy test.

1917—President Wilson vetoed literacy test a second time. Bill passed over veto by Senate and House.

1918—Clauses relating to literacy test lifted temporarily to allow admission of farm labor, principally from Mexico—a war measure.

1919—Bill to suspend immigration for four years not passed.

1920—Johnson bill suspending immigration for two years and setting 5 per cent limit based on number of each nationality already in the United States supplanted by Dillingham bill and passed.

Alien percentage reduced from 5 per cent to 3 per cent.

Bill did not secure President Wilson's signature.

1921—The act of May 19, 1921, restricting immigration from all countries (except British North America, Mexico, Central America, and South America) not subject to our laws and agreements regarding Orientals, to 3 per cent of the number of American citizens of each nation, resident in the United States, became operative on June 3, 1921.

Quotas for this percentage restriction based upon the census of 1910.

1922—Re-enactment of the Law of 1921 with slight modifications.

APPENDIX A

1924—New immigration law provided for quota allotments based upon 2 per cent of the census of 1890, instead of 3 per cent of the census of 1910.

Beginning July 1, 1927, quota of each nation to be established on the basis of the number which bears the same ratio to 150,000 as the number of inhabitants in continental United States having that national origin bears to the number of inhabitants in continental United States in 1920, but minimum quota of any nation will be 100.

Provision also made for issue of immigration certificates to prospective immigrants by our consuls abroad, eliminating to some extent embarrassments entailed in refusing admission of applicants after they have made a long journey across the ocean. Penalties for bringing immigrants without immigration certificates, or false certificates made extremely heavy.

A Recent Important Administrative Experiment

The Act of 1924 referred to in this appendix went into effect after the foregoing chapters were prepared. While it is a step in the direction of selective immigration, it does not provide the machinery necessary to make our policy more than superficially so. In the latter part of 1925, however, (as this book goes to press) a corps of several immigrant inspectors and Public Health officers has been detailed by administrative action for service at certain of the consulates located in the British Isles as "technical advisors" to American consular officers. This departure from old established custom was arranged by negotiations begun by the Secretary of Labor through official diplomatic channels whereby the consent of Great Britain and the Irish Free State were obtained to try out the plan experimentally. The plan of making primary examinations by immigrant and Public Health Service officers abroad has not been in operation long enough to determine its ultimate effect, but the results so far obtained have been more than gratifying not only to American officers, but to foreign representatives and nationals as well.

One of the objections raised to placing our selective machinery in ports of embarkation has been the statements made that foreign powers would resent the procedure as an interference with sovereign authority, but the consent of Great Britain and the Irish Free State to the administrative experiment is at least indicative of the attitude which might be assumed by other governments should Congress see fit to authorize and appropriate for an adequate and permanent staff of competent inspectors and physicians together with appropriate facilities in all emigration countries.

APPENDIX B

PERTINENT FACTS

1—36,000,000 people of this country are foreign-born or of foreign or mixed parentage.

2—Immigration by decades since 1820 has been as follows:

Year	Number	Year	Number
1821-1830....	143,439	1871-1880....	2,812,191
1831-1840....	599,125	1881-1890....	5,246,613
1841-1850....	1,713,251	1891-1900....	3,844,420
1851-1860....	2,598,214	1901-1910....	8,795,386
1861-1870....	2,314,824	1911-1920....	5,735,811

During this period almost 34,000,000 people immigrated to the United States.

3—Over 18,000,000 of these immigrants arrived since 1890.

4—During a recent year 297,000 aliens declared their intention to become American citizens.

5—In that same year 138,000 aliens were admitted to citizenship.

APPENDIX C

INCREASE OF POPULATION DUE TO IMMIGRATION

So far as immigration is concerned, the difference between the number of aliens admitted and departed is a measure of the annual increase of our alien population. This appendix includes a table showing the recent inward and outward movement of aliens. The official statistical records of aliens leaving the United States are only available since the year 1908.

The fact that the increase of our alien population in 1924 was so large is an evidence that a greater stability and permanence is given to immigration under the quasi restrictive policy represented by the quota limit law, according to the Commissioner General of Immigration in his report for that year.

The Commissioner General also calls attention to the following facts, shown by the table, concerning the trend of immigration and emigration during the period covered

1—The decidedly outward movement following the industrial depression of 1907.

2—The increase of both immigration and emigration after the signing of the armistice.

3—The decline of immigration in 1922 as a result of the quota limit law.

4—The revival of immigration under the quota act for the years 1923 and 1924.

5—The decline in emigration under the quota act for the years 1923 and 1924.

APPENDIX C

Net increase of population by arrival and departure of aliens, fiscal years ending June 30, 1908 to 1924

PERIOD	ADMITTED	DEPARTED	INCREASE
1908........................	924,695	714,828	209,867
1909........................	944,235	400,392	543,843
1910........................	1,198,037	380,418	817,619
Total 3 years, 1908-1910	3,066,967	1,495,638	1,571,329
1911........................	1,030,300	518,215	512,085
1912........................	1,017,155	615,292	401,863
1913....	1,427,227	611,924	815,303
1914........................	1,403,081	633,805	769,276
1915........................	434,244	384,174	50,070
1916........................	366,748	240,807	125,941
1917........................	362,877	146,379	216,498
1918........................	211,853	193,268	18,585
1919........................	237,021	216,231	20,790
1920........................	621,576	428,062	193,514
Total 10 years, 1911-1920	7,112,082	3,988,157	3,123,925
1921........................	978,163	426,031	552,132
1922........................	432,505	345,384	87,121
1923........................	673,406	200,586	472,820
1924................... ..	879,302	216,745	662,557
Total 4 years, 1921-1924	2,963,376	1,188,746	1,774,630
Grand total............	13,142,425	6,672,541	6,469,884

APPENDIX D

THE QUOTA LAWS

The old quota limit act of 1921, operative until June 30, 1924, provided that the number of aliens of any nationality admissible to the United States be limited to 3 per cent per year of the number of that particular nationality resident in the United States in 1910. Under this law the quotas of all countries for the fiscal year ending June 30, 1924, were exhausted with three exceptions, namely: Esthonia with a balance of 124 remaining of its quota, the Free State of Fiume with 5, and Iceland with 32. In studying the quota figures under the act of 1921 it should be borne in mind that:

1—The quota limit provision was not applicable to Canada, Mexico, and other parts of the New World.

2—The quotas allotted to the British Isles, Germany, and other northwestern countries were greater than the normal immigration from those countries.

The quota act of 1924 provides that "the annual quota of any nationality shall be 2 per cent of the number of foreign-born individuals of such nationality resident in continental United States as determined by the United States census of 1890, but the minimum quota of any nationality shall be 100."

APPENDIX D

The quotas from the various countries or regions of birth allotted under the old law of 1921 and the act of 1924 are shown below:

COUNTRY OR REGION OF BIRTH	ACT OF 1921	ACT OF 1924
Albania	288	100
Armenia (Russian)	230	124
Austria	7,342	785
Belgium	1,563	512
Bulgaria	302	100
Czechoslovakia	14,357	3,073
Danzig	301	228
Denmark	5,619	2,789
Esthonia	1,348	124
Finland	3,921	471
France	5,729	3,954
Germany	67,607	51,227
Great Britain, Ireland	77,342	34,007
Greece	3,063	100
Hungary	5,747	473
Iceland	75	100
Irish Free State*		28,567
Italy	42,057	3,845
Latvia	1,540	142
Lithuania	2,629	344
Luxemburg	92	100
Netherlands	3,607	1,648
Norway	12,202	6,453
Poland	30,977	5,982
Portugal	2,465	503
Rumania	7,419	603
Russia	24,405	2,248
Spain	912	131
Sweden	20,042	9,561
Switzerland	3,752	2,081
Yugoslavia	6,426	671
Palestine	57	100
Syria	882	100
Turkey	2,654	100
Australia	279	121
New Zealand and Pacific Islands	80	100
All Others	492	3,100
Total	357,803	164,667

*Included in Great Britain, Ireland, under Act of 1921.